English-Chinese 英汉对照

幽默集萃

A Collection of Humor

逸 云 选编

文匯出版社

图书在版编目(CIP)数据

英汉对照幽默集萃/逸云选编. —上海：文汇出版社，2008.1

ISBN 978-7-80741-281-6

Ⅰ.英… Ⅱ.逸… Ⅲ.①英语-汉语-对照读物②笑话-作品集-世界 Ⅳ.H319.4:I

中国版本图书馆 CIP 数据核字(2007)第 179868 号

英汉对照幽默集萃

选　　编 / 逸　云

责任编辑 / 陈今夫
特约编辑 / 文　夫
封面装帧 / 卓东东

出版发行 / 文汇出版社
上海市威海路 755 号
(邮政编码 200041)
经　　销 / 全国新华书店
照　　排 / 南京展望文化发展有限公司
印刷装订 / 上海长阳印刷厂
版　　次 / 2008 年 1 月第 1 版
印　　次 / 2008 年 1 月第 1 次印刷
开　　本 / 787×960　1/32
字　　数 / 90 千
印　　张 / 6.375
印　　数 / 1—8 000

ISBN 978-7-80741-281-6
定价：15.00 元

目录 Contents

I

Teacher and Pupil

老师与学生

Say Sir

Teacher: (to a new boy) What's your name, my little fellow?

New boy: David Smith.

Teacher: Always say "sir" please, when you are speaking to master. It's more polite.

New boy: (apologetically) Sir David Smith.

要叫先生

老师：（对一位新生说）小同学，你叫什么名字？

新生：我叫戴维·史密斯。

老师：请你跟老师说话时叫先生，这样比较有礼貌。

新生：（带歉意地）我叫戴维·史密斯先生。

* * *

Oxygen

The science teacher was explaining to the class, "Oxygen is necessary to all life. Without it there'd be no life at all. Now just think — it was only discovered about 100 years ago."

Mary raised her hand and asked, "If that's

true, what did people do before it was discovered?"

氧　气

自然科学老师在课堂上讲道:"氧气对任何生命都是必不可少的。如果没有氧气,地球上将不会有任何生命存在。大家想想——氧气的发现只有100多年。"

玛丽举起手问:"假如这是真的话,那么在氧气没被发现以前人类是怎么活着的?"

* * *

Gold

Professor: What happens to gold when it is exposed to the air?

Student (after reflection): It's stolen.

黄　金

教授: 黄金暴露在空气中会如何?

学生(思考以后): 被偷。

* * *

A Physics Examination

Once in a physics examination, Mike finished

the first question very soon, while his classmates were thinking it hard.

The question was: When it thouders why do we see the lightning first, then hear the thunderrolls?

Mike's answer: Because our eyes are before ears.

一次物理考试

在一次物理考试时，当同学们都还在苦思冥想时，麦克很快就答好了第一个问题。

这个问题是：为什么在打雷时，我们总是先看到闪电后听到雷声？

麦克的回答是：因为眼睛在前，耳朵在后。

* * *

Three Reasons

Teacher: Harry, give me three reasons why you know the Earth to be round.

Harry: Ma says so, Pa says so, and you say so!

三 条 理 由

老师：哈里，说出三条理由来证实地球是圆的。

哈里：妈妈是这么说的，爸爸是这么说的，你也是这么说的!

*　　*　　*

When Do People Talk Least?

Student A：When do people talk least?

Student B：In February.

Student A：Why?

Student B：Because February is the shortest month of a year.

人们什么时候说话最少?

学生甲：人们在什么时候说话最少?

学生乙：在二月。

学生甲：为什么呢?

学生乙：因为二月是一年中最短的一个月。

*　　*　　*

Guessing a Riddle

Teacher：Boys，I have a riddle to ask you. There's something wearing beautiful feather，and it can wake you up every morning. What is it，Jack?

Jack：A feather duster，with which father wakes me up every morning.

猜 谜

老师：孩子们，我有个谜语要你们猜：有一种东西，浑身都是漂亮的羽毛，每天早晨它能叫你起床。那是什么东西，杰克？

杰克：鸡毛掸子，爸爸每天都用它叫我起床。

* * *

Columbus' Telephone Number

Little Kathy: I find in my history book there is always such number (1451 - 1506) after the name Christopher Cloumbus. Would you please explain why, sir?

Little Linda: I can tell her, sir. It was Columbus' telephone number!

哥伦布的电话号码

小凯茜：我在历史书中发现，克里斯托弗·哥伦布这个名字后老是有(1451—1506)这几个数字。老师，请您给解释一下好吗？

小琳达：老师，我能告诉她。那是哥伦布的电话号码！

* * *

Visiting a Chicken Farm

One day, a teacher took his pupils to a chicken farm to pay a visit. When they came near the incubator, a chick just got out of its eggshell.

"It's wonderful to see a little thing come out from the eggshell, isn't it?" the teacher said.

"Yes, sir," said one of the boys, "But it would be more wonderful if we knew that how a chick gets into its eggshell before hand."

参观养鸡场

一天,老师带学生到养鸡场参观,当他们走近孵化器时,刚好一只小鸡破壳而出。

"看见一个小生命从蛋壳里出来,岂不是很奇妙的吗?"老师说。

"是的,老师,"一个男学生说,"可是,如果我们知道它是怎样事先钻进蛋壳里的,那就更奇妙了。"

* * *

The Composition Class

The students in the composition class were assigned the task of writing an essay on "the most beautiful thing I ever saw." The student who, of all the members of the class, seemed the least sensitive to beauty, handed in his paper first with astonishing speed. It was short and to the point. He had written:

"The most beautiful thing I ever saw was too beautiful for words."

作 文 课

在作文课上,学生们被布置写一篇题为"我所见到过的最美的东西"的文章。在整个班级中看起来对美最不敏感的那个学生用令人吃惊的速度第一个交了卷。这篇作文短而扼要。他写道:"我所见到过的最美的东西,美得无法用语言来表达。"

* * *

Writing a Composition

One day in class, the teacher assigned his students to write a composition — If I Am a Manager.

All the students began to write except a boy. The teacher went to him and asked the reason.

"I am waiting for my secretary," was the boy's answer.

写 作 文

一天课上，老师要同学们以“如果我是一个经理”为题写一篇作文。所有的学生都在动笔写了，只有一个男生例外。老师走过去问他为什么不写。

“我在等我的秘书”。那孩子答道。

* * *

The Same Mother

John and his brother Peter were in the same class. The teacher assigned them to write a composition “My Mother”. Peter wrote one and John just copied it.

On the next day the teacher asked John, “How is it that your composition is exactly the same with Peter's?”

“We have the same mother, don't we?” replied John.

同一个妈妈

约翰和他的哥哥彼得在同一个班里上学，一天老师布置他们写一篇作文，题目是“我的妈妈”。彼得写好后约翰拿去抄了一遍。

第二天老师问约翰:“为什么你的作文和彼得的一模一样?”

约翰回答说:“我们的妈妈是同一个人,不是吗?”

* * *

Very Long Absence

“Good morning, Jimmy,” said the history teacher, “I see you are back at last. Are you better?”

“Yes, thank you, sir.”

“Good, now how long were you away?”

“Since the Crusades, sir.”

长时间缺席

“早上好,吉米,”历史老师说,“我终于看到你又回到了学校。你身体好些了吗?”

“好些了,谢谢您,老师。”

“很好,你是什么时候开始缺课的?”

“老师,从‘十字军东征’的时候。”

* * *

Who Discovered Australia?

Teacher: Find Australia on the map for me,

Eddie.

Eddie: It's there, sir.

Teacher: That's right. Now Benny, who discovered Australia?

Benny: Eddie, sir.

谁发现了澳洲?

老师:埃迪,在地图上给我找出澳洲在什么地方。

埃迪:先生,在这儿。

老师:对了。本尼,你来回答我是谁发现了澳洲?

本尼:先生,是埃迪。

*　　*　　*

Overcrowded Moon

A geography teacher once told her class, "The moon is so large that several million people could live there."

One boy started laughing, "It sure must get crowded when it's a crescent moon."

拥挤的月亮

一位地理老师告诉他的学生:"月亮非常大,可以容纳几百万人在上面居住。”

有个男孩笑了，“当月亮由满月变成月牙时，住在上面的人一定很拥挤。”

* * *

He Knows the Answer

Teacher: Can you tell me anything about the great scientists of the 18th century?

Pupil: Yes, sir, I can. They are all dead.

他知道答案

教师：你能告诉我一些有关 18 世纪的伟大科学家的事情吗？

学生：我能，先生。他们都死了。

* * *

An Unexpected Answer

Teacher: What do elephants have that no other animals have?

Pupil: Little elephants.

出乎意料的回答

老师：什么东西只有大象才有，其他动物都没有？

小学生：小象。

*　　*　　*

Apples

Teacher：Now if you had five apples in your pocket，could I take seven out?

Lanny：No，sir.

Teacher：That's correct，and why not?

Lanny：Because they're not yours.

苹　果

老师：现在如果你口袋里有5个苹果，我能拿出7个吗？

兰尼：不行，老师。

老师：对了。为什么不行呢？

兰尼：因为它们不是你的。

*　　*　　*

Chocolate

Teacher：If you had five chocolate bars，and your younger sister asked you for one，how many would you have left?

Terry：Five!

巧克力

老师：假如你有五块巧克力，你妹妹问你要一块，你还剩几块？

特里：还剩五块！

* * *

To Go to Heaven

Sunday School teacher: Hands up all those who want to go to Heaven? Hands up... what about you, Tom? You haven't got your hand up — don't you want to go to Heaven?

Tom: I can't. My Mum told me to go straight home.

去天堂

主日学校的教员：想去天堂的人举起手来。把手举起来……你呢，汤姆？你还没举手呢——你不想去天堂吗？

汤姆：我去不了，因为妈妈让我一放学就回家。

* * *

Correct

Teacher：Bobby，what are the three words which pupils use most often at school?

Bobby：I don't know . . .

Teacher：Correct.

很　对

教师：鲍比，学生在学校里经常用的三个字是什么？

鲍比：不知道……

教师：很对。

*　　*　　*

Whose Fault

Teacher：Annie，you made so many mistakes in your exercises，surely your mother will blame you!

Annie：Blame me？Oh，no. On the contrary，I'll blame her，because it was she that did my homework instead.

谁 的 错

老师：安妮，你作业中出了这么多错，你妈妈一定会责怪你的!

安妮:责怪我?啊,不会的。正相反,我倒要责怪她呢,是她替我做的作业。

*　*　*

Mixed Doubles

Teacher of Physical Education : Have you ever seen mixed doubles, boys?

Davy: Yes, sir. Quite often. I saw it even last night.

Teacher: Please tell us something about it.

Davy: Oh, sorry, sir. My father always says, "Domestic shame should not be published."

混 合 双 打

体育老师:孩子们,你们见过男女混合双打吗?

戴维:见过,老师,经常见。就在昨天夜里我还见过呢?

老师:你给大家讲讲当时的情形吧。

戴维:啊,对不起,老师。我爸爸常说,"家丑不可外扬。"

*　*　*

The Biggest in the World

Hans dozed off while his teacher was talking.

Teacher: Hans! Tell us, what's the biggest in the world?

Hans: Well, well ... eyelids ...

Teacher: What? Eyelids?

Hans: Yes, sir. Because as soon as I shut my eyes, the eyelids cover everything of the world.

世界上最大的

老师正在讲课,汉斯打起瞌睡来了。

老师:汉斯!你说说,世界上什么最大?

汉斯:这,这……眼皮……

老师:什么?眼皮?

汉斯:是这样,老师,因为我眼睛一闭,眼皮就把世界上的一切东西都遮住了。

* * *

An Absolute Zero

Student: I don't think I deserve an absolute zero.

Professor: Neither do I, but it is the lowest mark that I am allowed to give.

零　分

学生：我认为我不应该得零分。

教授：我也这么认为，但这是允许我打的最低分数。

*　　*　　*

Swim

Teacher：I hear you live close to the river and yet you never learned to swim?

Sammy：What's so strange about that? You're surrounded by air，yet you can't fly!

游　泳

老师：我听说你家住的离河很近，可你竟然没学会游泳。

萨米：这有什么好奇怪的？你被空气包围着，可你也不会飞啊！

*　　*　　*

The Dean's Words

Student A：If the Dean doesn't take back what he said to me this morning，I am going to leave college.

Student B：What did he say?

Student A：He told me to leave college.

院长的话

学生甲：如果院长不收回他今天早上对我说的话，我就离开学院。

学生乙：他说了什么？

学生甲：他要我退学。

*　　*　　*

I Am My Father

One day little Jack didn't want to go to school and telephoned the teacher pretended to be his father and said, "Hello. Is that the teacher speaking? My little Jack caught cold today and he can't go to school. He asked me to ask you for a day's leave."

The teacher at the other end of the telephone asked, "Who is that speaking?"

"It's my father, sir," answered Jack.

是我爸爸

一天，杰克不想去上学，就装成爸爸的声调给老师打电话。他说："喂，你好，你是老师吧？我的小杰克感冒了，不能去上学，他让我向您请一天假。"

老师问道："您是谁？"

杰克回答道："是我爸爸，先生。"

*　　*　　*

A Bad Tooth

Teacher: Roy, why weren't you in school yesterday?

Roy: I had a bad tooth, miss.

Teacher: Oh, I'm sorry to hear that. Is it better now?

Roy: Don't Know, miss. I left it with the dentist.

牙　疼

老师：罗伊，你昨天怎么没来上课？

罗伊：小姐，我昨天牙疼。

老师：噢，真可怜。现在好点儿了吗？

罗伊：我不知道，我把它留在牙医那儿了。

*　　*　　*

Father's John Hancock

Teacher: Kenny, you haven't shown your parents the examination papers, have you?

Kenny: Yes, I have, sir.

Teacher: But I can't find your father's John Hancock on the papers at all.

Kenny: Here, sir. (showing his whipped arms to the teacher.)

父亲的亲笔签名

老师:肯尼,你没把你的考卷给父母看,是吗?

肯尼:不,老师,我给看了。

老师:可是我在上面根本没找着你父亲的签名啊。

肯尼:在这里,老师。(肯尼向老师露出手臂上的鞭伤。)

* * *

Class and Ass

Professor Depew of Glasgow put his notice on his door: "Professor Depew will not meet his classes today."

A student, after reading the notice, rubbed

out the “c”.

Later Professor Depew came along, and entering into the spirit of the joke, rubbed out the “l”.

班和笨驴

格拉斯哥的迪普教授在门上贴了这样一个通知:“迪普教授今天不见他的班级。”

一个学生读了通知后,擦掉了字母“c”(lass:姑娘)。

后来迪普教授来了,也想开开玩笑,他擦掉了字母“l”(ass:笨驴)。

* * *

On Miracle

In Sunday school, the minister was trying to illustrate the word miracle. “Boys and girls,” he said, “suppose I stood on the roof of a ten-story building, lost my balance and fell off. Then all of a sudden in midair, a whirlwind swept me up and brought me safely to the ground. Now what word would you use to describe this?”

After a long silence a boy raised his hand and said, “Luck?”

"True, true," replied the minister. "It could be luck — but that's not the word I wanted. I'll repeat the story. There I am on top of the ten-story building again, and I fall. A whirlwind catches me in midair and places me safely on the ground. Think now — what word would decribe the situation?"

"Accident," cried out one girl.

"No, no," answered the minister. "Listen carefully for the third time. I'm on the same building; I fall and am swept to safety by a sudden whirlwind. What word could account for my safely reaching the ground?"

The boys and girls shouted in unison: "Practice!"

论 奇 迹

在主日学校里，牧师正举例说明“奇迹”一词的意义。“孩子们，”他说：“假如我站在一座十层高的楼顶上，失去平衡掉了下来。在跌落到半空中时，突然刮来一阵旋风，把我举起来，使我安全着陆。想想看，该用什么词来描绘这件事？”

很长时间没有回答。后来一个男孩举手说：“运气。”

“好吧，好吧，”牧师回答说：“可以说是运气，不过那不是我想要的词。我再讲一遍这个故事。我还是在一座十层高的楼顶上,从上面摔下来。一阵旋风在半空中把我托住,使我安全返回地面。好好想一下,该用什么词来描绘这一情景呢?"

"意外。"有个女孩大声说。

"不对,不对,"牧师说:"你们仔细听,再听一遍。我还是在那座楼顶上,摔下来时被一阵突然刮来的旋风托住,转危为安。用什么词来解释我安全返回地面这事?"

孩子们齐声叫道:"反复练习!"

II

Lovers and Couples

情侣夫妻

Who Were the Other Two?

An adjective has three qualitative degrees: good, better and best.

The pernickety English grammar teacher married a man of quality. "You are the best woman in my life," announced the groom on their wedding night.

"And just who were the other two?" angrily snapped the grammar-conscious bride.

另外两个是谁?

一个形容词有三个程度上的级别：好的，比较好的和最好的。

一位爱挑剔的英语语法老师嫁了一位上等绅士。新郎在新婚之夜宣称："你是我一生中遇到的最好的女人。"

这位语法概念很清楚的新娘生气地问："那么另外两个是谁?"

* * *

Christmas Cards

A young man approached the counter at which Christmas cards were being sold.

"Have you anything sentimental?" he asked.

"Here's a lovely one," replied the salesgirl. "to the Only Girl I Ever Loved."

"That's fine, I'll take four... no... six of those please."

圣诞卡片

一位年轻人来到卖圣诞卡片的柜台前面。

"你们这儿有表达情意绵绵的卡片吗?"他问道。

"这张比较可爱,"女售货员答道,上面写道"赠给我唯一心爱的姑娘。"

"太好了,请给我拿四张,不,六张。"

* * *

A Definition

At a women's meeting we were discussing philosophy, and the pastor's wife read this definition:"A philosopher is a person who talks about something he doesn't understand, and makes you think it's your fault." The woman next to me turned and whispered, "I thought that was a husband!"

定 义

在一次妇女集会上，我们讨论哲学。一位牧师的妻子给大家读了一段定义：“哲学家就是这样一种人，他谈论自己都不懂的东西，反而使你认为你不懂是自己的过错。”坐在我旁边的一位夫人跟我耳语道：“我还以为这是丈夫的定义呢。”

* * *

Under the Weather

The old gentleman came to breakfast wobbly and bleary-eyed. As he sugared his coffee, his wife noticed his bandaged hand and asked for an explanation.

"It was a matter of small consequence at our club's banquet last night, my dear," he told her. "You see, some of the younger men who can't handle their liquor got a little under the weather. And one of them, well, stepped on my hand."

喝醉了酒

一位老绅士摇摇晃晃，醉眼惺忪地下楼来吃早点。当他往咖啡里加糖时，妻子发现他的手上缚着绷带，应问他怎么回事。

“亲爱的，事情是这样的，昨晚在我们俱乐部的晚宴上出了点小乱子，造成这个结果。”他告诉她。“你知道，有些年轻小伙子酒量不大，喝几口就晕了头。有一个一脚就踩到我手上了。”

*　*　*

A Never Finished Job

I was going away for a few days and left my husband a list of chores. For fun, I put down as Item 5: Think about your wife a lot.

After I returned, my husband proudly reported that he had completed every job. When I saw the list, however, each item except No. 5 had been crossed off. “What's this!” I exclaimed, “Didn't you think about me while I was gone?”

My chagrin vanished when he replied cheerfully, “I started to, but just never finished.”

一直没干完的活

我离开家几天，给丈夫留了个条儿，写下需要做的杂活。为了跟他逗着玩儿，我的第五条写的是：多想念你的妻子。

当我回来后，我丈夫非常自豪地向我汇报，他干完了所有的活。当我看条子时，除了第五条，所有的活都干完划掉了,“这是怎么回事!”我惊叫道,“我不在时,你不想我吗?”

他高兴地说:“我开始干了,不过这活一直还没做完。”这时我的委曲都消失了。

* * *

Whose Profession?

A lawyer and his wife were walking down the street when a luscious blonde waved to the lawyer, and threw him a kiss. His annoyed wife asked him who the girl was and he said: “She's just a woman I met last week, professionally of course.” Rigidly, the wife asked: “Whose profession? Yours or hers?”

谁的职业?

一个律师和他太太正走在街上时,有个甜美的金发女郎向律师招手,并抛来一个飞吻。他气恼的太太问他那女郎是谁时,他说:“她只是我上星期遇到的女人,当然是职业上的。”太太严厉地问:“谁的职业?你的?还是她的?”

* * *

If I Were Your Husband

"Winston, if you were my husband, I'd put poison in your coffee." "Nancy," replied Churchill, "if I were your husband, I'd drink that coffee."

如果我是你丈夫

"温斯顿,如果你是我丈夫,我会放毒药在你的咖啡里。""南茜,"丘吉尔回答说,"如果我是你丈夫,我会喝下那咖啡。"

*　　*　　*

Give Him Another Chance

Husband: I am going to discharge our chauffeur. Four times recently he almost killed me.

Wife: Darling, give him another chance.

再给他一次机会

丈夫:我要解雇我们的司机。最近有 4 次他差点害死我。

妻子:亲爱的,再给他一次机会。

*　　*　　*

Dream

"My wife had a funny dream last night," confided a man to his companion. "She dreamed she had married a multimillionaire." "You're lucky," sighed the companion. "My wife dreams that in the daytime."

做 梦

"我太太昨天晚上做了个可笑的梦,"一个男人对他的同伴透露说,"她梦到她嫁了个亿万富翁。""你很幸运,"同伴叹息地说,"我太太在白天做梦。"

* * *

Keeping Up with the Joneses

Emily was the kind of wife who had to keep up with the Joneses.

"Dear," complained Herbert. "Aren't you getting a little greedy in trying to keep up with the neighbors?"

"I don't know what you mean," Emily answered.

"First the Smith family bought a new refrigerator, so we had to buy one, too."

"Well, our refrigerator was already five years old."

"Then the Crisp family bought a color TV console and you insisted we needed one."

"Our nineteen-inch color set was too small."

"Later the Brang family bought a new car and we had to buy a new car. Why do we have to keep up with the Joneses?"

"We're just as good as our neighbors," Emily retaliated.

"Well, I have news for you."

"Yes?"

"The Culp family just had quintuplets."

和邻居攀比

艾米莉是那种偏要和邻居攀比的太太。

"亲爱的,"赫伯特抱怨说,"你试着要和邻居们攀比,不是有点贪心吗?"

"我不知道你是什么意思。"艾米莉回答。

"首先史密斯家买了一台新的冰箱,所以我们也得买一台。"

"嗯,我们的冰箱已经用了 5 年。"

"然后克里斯波家买了一台落地式彩色电视机,你就坚持我们需要一台。"

"我们 19 英寸的彩色电视机太小了。"

"后来布来格家买了辆新车,而我们也得买一辆,为什么我们得和邻居攀比?"

"我们只不过和邻居一样好而已,"艾米莉回敬一句。

"那么我要告诉你一件新闻。"

"什么?"

"科尔波家刚生了五胞胎。"

* * *

An Old Couple's Quarrel

A couple of codgers got into a quarrel and came before the local magistrate. The loser, turning to his opponent in a combative frame of mind, cried: "I'll law you to the Circuit Court."

"I'm willing," said the other.

"I'll law you to the Supreme Court."

"I'll be there."

"And I'll law the hell!"

"My attorney will be there," was the calm reply.

老夫妻吵架

一对性情乖僻的老夫妻发生了争吵,一直闹到地方法官那里。败诉的一方以一种临战的姿态冲着对方嚷道:“我要到巡回法庭去告你。”

“愿意奉陪。”另一个说。

“我要到最高法院去告你。”

“我也陪你。”

“我还要到地狱去告你。”

“我的代理人会奉陪的。”对方平静地说。

* * *

I wish I were a newspaper

Wife talking to her husband, who reads newspaper all day: I wish I were a newspaper so I'll be in your hands all day.

Husband: I wish that too, so I could change you daily.

我要是报纸就好了

妻子和丈夫谈话,他一天到晚总是看报纸,妻子抱怨说:我要是报纸就好了,那样我就可以天天在你手里了。

丈夫说我也希望那样,那样我就可以每天换一个了。

* * *

Roulette

At a gambling casino, a husband gave his wife, who had never played roulette, $50 to bet. When she asked what number she should play, a friend suggested that she choose her age as a possible number.

She placed $25 on 28. The ball rolled round and landed on 32. The lady promptly fainted.

轮 盘 赌

在一家赌场里，一个丈夫给他从未赌过轮盘的妻子 50 美元去赌。当她问说应该选几号时，一个朋友建议她选她年龄的号码。

她把 25 美元放在 28 上。那球旋转着，停在 32 上。女人立刻昏了过去。

* * *

The Same Service

A man who had been married for ten years was consulting a marriage counselor.

"When I was first married, I was very happy. I'd come home from a hard day down at the shop, and my little dog would race around barking, and my wife would bring me my slippers. Now everything's changed. When I come home, my dog brings me my slippers, and my wife barks at me."

"I don't know what you're complaining about," said the counselor, "You're still getting the same service."

同样的服务

有位结婚十年的男人,正向婚姻顾问请教。

"新婚时我非常幸福。在市区的商店里累了一天,回到家里,小狗围着我又跑又叫,妻子忙给我拿来拖鞋。现在一切都变了。小狗给我叼来拖鞋,妻子对我又喊又叫。"

"我不知道你有什么可抱怨的,"顾问说,"你得到的服务还是同样的嘛。"

* * *

I Don't Know Her

A couple walking in the park noticed a young man and woman sitting on a bench, passionately kissing.

"Why don't you do that?" said the wife.

"Honey," replied her husband, "I don't

even know that woman!"

我还不认识她呢

一对夫妇在公园里散步,发现一对年轻的男女坐在一条长凳上,动情地接吻。

"你为什么不那么做呢?"妻子说。

"亲爱的,"丈夫回答说,"我还不认识那个女子呢!"

*　　*　　*

How Much Is It?

It was winter, and Mrs. Waterman wanted to do a lot of shopping, so she waited until it was Saturday, when her husband was free, and she took him to the shops with her to pay for everything and to carry her parcels. They went to a lot of shops, and Mrs. Waterman bought a lot of things. She often stopped and said, "Look, Joe! Isn't that beautiful!"

He then answered, "All right, dear, How much is it?" and took his money out to pay for it.

It was dark when they came out of the last shop, and Mr. Waterman was tired and thinking about other things, like a nice drink by the side of a warm fire at home. Suddenly his wife looked up at the sky and said, "Look at that beautiful moon, Joe!"

Without stopping, Mr. Waterman answered, "All right, dear, How much is it?"

多 少 钱?

严冬来临,瓦特曼太太想采购一大批东西,所以她就一直等到周六丈夫有空的时候,她拖着他去商店付钱连带拎包裹。他们去了许多商店,瓦特曼太太买了一大堆东西。她经常停下脚步说道:"看,乔伊!那个多漂亮!"

他总是回答:"好吧!亲爱的,多少钱?"然后掏钱去付款。

他们从最后一家商店出来的时候夜幕已经降临,瓦特曼先生已筋疲力尽了。他心里想着其他事情,比如在家里暖暖的火炉边呷口美酒。突然他太太仰望天空,说道:"看那月亮多美,乔伊!"

瓦特曼先生不假思索答道:"好吧,亲爱的,多少钱?"

* * *

Relative By Marriage

A husband and wife drove for miles in silence

after a terrible argument in which neither would budge. The husband pointed to a mule in a pasture.

"Relative of yours?" he asked.

"Yes," she replied. "By marriage."

婆家的亲戚

一对夫妻开着车出去,走了很长一段时间谁也不吭声。因为在这之前他们曾争吵得很厉害,谁也不肯让步。丈夫指着牧场上的一头骡子问道:"是你的亲戚吗?"

"是的,"她回答,"是婆家的亲戚。"

* * *

A Family Quarrel

The young newly-weds quarreled. At last she could bear it no longer and burst into tears.

"I don't want to have anything to do with you any more. I'm packing up my things and going off to mother."

"Fine, my dear," said the husband. "Here are the travelling expenses."

She counted the money. "What about the money for the return ticket?"

家庭的争吵

一对年轻的新婚夫妇吵架了。最后妻子终于忍不住哭了起来。

“我要跟你吹了。我要去收拾东西,离开这里回娘家去。”

“好,亲爱的,”丈夫说,“给你路费。”

她数了数钱。“还有回来的路费呢?”

*　　*　　*

My Husband Will Be Home Soon

A married man was visiting his “girlfriend” when she requested that he shave his beard.

“Oh Ralph, I like your beard, but I would really love to see your handsome face.”

Ralph replied, “My wife loves this beard, I couldn't possibly do it, she would kill me!!”

“Oh please?” the girlfriend asked again, in a sexy little voice ...

“Oh really, I can't,” he replies ... “My wife loves this beard!!”

The girlfriend asked once more, and he sighs and finally gives in. That night Ralph crawls into bed with his wife while she was sleeping.

The wife is awakened somewhat, feels his face and replies "Oh Michael, you shouldn't be here, my husband will be home soon!"

我丈夫马上就要回来了

一个已婚男人去拜访他的"女朋友"时,女朋友要求他剃去胡须。

"噢,拉尔夫,我喜欢你的胡子,但我更喜欢看到你英俊的面孔。"

拉尔夫回答说,"我的妻子喜欢我的胡子,所以我不可能剃掉它,否则她会杀了我的。"

"噢,我求你了,"女朋友用一种低沉的、性感的声音又一次说道。

"可是,我不能,"他回答道,"我的妻子喜欢这胡子。"

在女朋友再三请求下,他终于屈服同意了。夜里,在妻子熟睡时,拉尔夫爬上了床。

妻子朦朦胧胧地摸了摸他的脸说道,"噢,米歇尔,你不应该在这里,我的丈夫很快就要回来了。"

* * *

Golf Balls

A young couple gets married, and the groom asks his bride if he can have a dresser drawer of his own that she will never open. The bride agrees. After 30 years of marriage, she notices that his drawer has been left open. She peeks inside and ses three golf balls and $1,000.

She confronts her husband and asks for an explanation. He explains, "Every time I was unfaithful to you, I put a golf ball in the drawer." She figures three times in 30 years isn't bad and asks, "But what about the $1,000?" He replied, "Whenever I got a dozen golf balls, I sold them."

高尔夫球

有一对年轻人结婚了，新郎问新娘，他是否可以拥有一个属于他自己装衣服的抽屉，而新娘永远不要打开。新娘同意了。结婚 30 年后，妻子注意到，她丈夫的抽屉是开着的，她往里瞥了一眼，看见里面有三个高尔夫球和 1 000 美元。

她质问丈夫，并要求解释。丈夫解释道："每次我不忠于你的时候，我就往抽屉里放一个高尔夫球。"她想，30 年来才 3 次，还不是太坏。于是便问："那么 1 000 美元是怎么回事呢?"丈夫回答说："我一攒够 12 个高尔夫球，就把它们卖了。"

* * *

S.O.B.

My father, who was 14 years old than my mother, had been working on his will. At a family dinner he told us that he had provided well for Mother, but the family home would go to us five children if she remarried.

"I don't want another S. O. B. toasting his shins around my fireplace," he explained.

With a sly grin, Mother cracked, "What makes you think I'd marry another S. O. B?"

狗娘养的

我爸比我妈大 14 岁，最近一直在写遗嘱。一次家宴上，他告诉我们说他为母亲以后的生活作好了安排，但如果她改嫁的话，家里的房子将归我们五个孩子所有。

"我可不愿意另外哪个狗娘养的在我的火炉旁烤他的狗腿，"他解释道。

妈妈狡猾地咧了咧嘴，讥诮道："你怎么认为我会再嫁给一个狗娘养的？"

* * *

Gardening Gloves

For months I hinted that I needed a new wedding ring, since I had developed an allergy to gold. On my birthday, while I was gardening, my husband asked me for gift suggestions. I held my hands up and said, "Well, you'll notice that my hands are bare."

Later that evening I opened my present with enthusiasm. "Happy birthday," he said, as I unwrapped a new pair of gardening gloves.

园艺手套

几个月以来,我一直在向丈夫暗示我需要一枚新的结婚戒指,因为我对黄金有点过敏。生日那天,我正在干园艺活时,丈夫问我想要什么礼物。我举起双手说:"嗯,你肯定看到了,我的两手都是光光的。"

那天晚上,我满怀热情地拆开了丈夫送的礼物。"生日快乐!"他说。我打开一看:里面包着一双园艺手套。

Ⅲ

Parents and children

父母与孩子

Thinking Back

We were gathered together, all ten of us, for our widowed mother's 80th birthday. The conversation was of early struggles, walking to work and saving up in clothing clubs, when my elder sister said, "Of course, we were bound to be poor because we were such a big family. Mom, why did you have so many children?"

Mother looked around at us all and said, "Well where did you want me to stop?"

回　忆

我们总共十个人,聚在一起祝贺已成为寡妇的妈妈的八十岁生日。谈的话题是我们家早年的挣扎,走着去上班,在"新衣会"里存钱准备买衣裳。这时我姐姐说:"当然,我们的生活没有法子不艰难,因为我们家孩子太多了。妈妈,您为什么要生这么多的孩子?"

妈妈看了我们一圈说:"那么,你想让我在哪儿停住呢?"

* * *

What'll I do?

A friend was trying to encourage his elderly

mother to enjoy the money she had accumulated through frugal living. "Mother," he said, "you have enough money to last you until you're a hundred."

"And then what'll I do?" she replied.

我以后怎么办?

我一位朋友试图说服他年老的妈妈,用她一辈子过俭朴生活储存下来的钱享受一下。"妈妈,"他说,"您那些钱足够您享用到一百岁了。"

"那么以后我该怎么办呢?"她问道。

* * *

You Will Save Much More

"You will be pleased with me today, mother," said Dick to his mother, coming home from school. "I saved on fares. I didn't go to school by bus, I ran all the way after it."

"Well," said his mother laughing, "Next time you should run after a taxi, you will save much more."

你会省得更多

"妈妈,你今天一定会对我满意的,"迪克放学回家后对妈妈说,“我省下了车钱。我上学时没乘公共汽车,而是跟着公共汽车一路跑到学校的。”

“哦,”他妈妈笑着说,“下次你跟在出租汽车后面跑,那会省得更多。”

*　　*　　*

I Taught the Teacher

Mother asked her little boy, “Darling, what did the teacher teach you today?”

“Nothing, Mum,” answered the son proudly, “instead, she asked me how much one plus two was, and l told her three.”

我 教 老 师

妈妈问她的小儿子:“宝贝儿,今天老师都教你些什么?”

儿子骄傲地说:“什么也没教,妈妈,她反倒问我一加二等于几,我告诉她是三。”

*　　*　　*

The Result of Laziness

Mother: Why were you kept after school today, Tommy?

Tommy: Teacher told us to write an essay on "The Result of Laziness", and I turned in a blank sheet of paper.

懒惰的结果

妈妈:汤米,你今天放学以后为什么被留下了?

汤米:老师叫我们写一篇题为"懒惰的结果"的作文,我交了一张白卷。

* * *

Who Is the Laziest?

Father: Well, Boby, I talked to your teacher today, and now I want to ask you a question. Who is the laziest person in your class?

Boby: I don't know, father.

Father: Oh, yes, you do! Think! When other boys and girls are doing and writing, who sits in the class and only watches how other people work?

Boby: Our teacher, father.

谁 最 懒?

父亲:哎,鲍比,今天我跟你们老师谈过,现在我想问你个问题,你们班上谁最懒?

鲍比：我不知道，爸爸。

父亲：啊，不对，你知道！想想看，当别的孩子们都在做作业、写字时，谁在课堂上坐着，只是看人家做功课？

鲍比：我们老师，爸爸。

*　　*　　*

Conduct and Courtesy

Father: The school report gives you a D for conduct and an A for courtesy. How did you manage that?

Herbert: Whenever I punch someone, I apologize.

品德与礼貌

父亲：学校的成绩单上给你的品德分是D，礼貌分是A，你这是怎么搞的？

赫伯特：无论我什么时候打了人，过后我都会向人家道歉的。

*　　*　　*

To Learn French

Son: Dad, is French difficult to learn?

Father：My boy，at the beginning it is，but after that it becomes easy.

Son：That's great！I'll learn the latter half.

学 法 语

儿子：爸爸，法语难学吗？

父亲：我的孩子，开头是难，可往后就变得容易了。

儿子：太好了！那我就学后半部分。

* * *

Tom's History Examination

Aunt：How did Tom do his history examination?

Mother：Oh，not at all well，but there，it wasn't his fault. Why，they asked him things that happened before the poor boy was born.

汤姆的历史考试

姨妈：汤姆这孩子历史考得怎么样？

母亲：唉，糟透了。可话又说回来，这也不能怪他。嗨，他们尽问一些这个可怜的孩子出生前的事情。

* * *

Each Other

Co-worker: "So you're the father of twins. Who do they look like?"

Excited parent: "Each other."

互 相 像

同事:"这么说,你得了一对双胞胎,当了父亲。他们看起来长得像谁?"

激动的父亲:"他们互相像。"

* * *

Children's Faults

"It is extraordinary that Mrs. Brown can never see any faults in her children," said Mrs. Smith. "Mothers never can," remarked her husband.

"What an absurd idea, James! So like a man, I'm sure I should see faults in our children at once — if they had any."

孩子的缺点

史密斯太太说:"多奇怪啊,布朗太太从来看不见她孩子的缺点。"

“做母亲的都是这样，”她丈夫回答。

“詹姆斯，这是多荒谬的说法！我相信，我和男人一样，我孩子的缺点我一眼就能看出来——如果他们有缺点的话。”

* * *

The Result of a Promise

Father：I promised to buy you a car if you passed your examination，and you have failed. What were you doing last term?

Son：I was learning to drive a car.

许诺的结果

父亲：我曾向你许诺，如果考试及格就给你买辆小汽车，可你却未能做到。你上学期一直在干什么呀？

儿子：我在学开汽车。

* * *

The Father and His Son

Father：You know，Jim，when Lincoln was your age，he was a very good pupil. In fact，he was the best pupil in his class.

Jim: Yes, Father. I know that. But when he was your age, he was Presedent of the United States.

父 与 子

父亲：吉姆，你要知道，当林肯在你这年龄时，他是一个很好的学生。事实上，他是班里最好的学生。

吉姆：是的，爸爸，我知道。可当他在你这个年龄时，他已是美国总统了。

* * *

Comparison

Jonny says to his father (who is looking at his son's report card). "So I don't get the highest marks in the class, do you get the highest salary in the office?"

比 较

乔尼对爸爸说(爸爸正在看儿子的成绩单)："我在班里没有拿到最高的成绩，那你在单位里拿到最高的薪水了吗？"

* * *

Drunk

One day, a father and his little son were going home. At this age, the boy was interested in all kinds of things and was always asking questions. Now, he asked, "What's the meaning of the word 'Drunk', dad?"

"Well, my son," his father replied, "look, there are standing two policemen. If I regard the two policemen as four then I am drunk."

"But, dad," the boy said, "there's only ONE policeman!"

醉 酒

一天,父亲与小儿子一道回家。这孩子正处于那种对什么事都很感兴趣的年龄,老是有提不完的问题。他向父亲发问道:"爸爸,'醉'字是什么意思?"

"唔,孩子,"父亲回答说,"你瞧那儿站着两个警察。如果我把他们看成了四个,那么我就算醉了。"

"可是,爸爸,"孩子说,"那儿只有一个警察呀!"

* * *

Big Head

"All the kids make fun of me," the boy cried to his mother. "They say I have a big head."

"Don't listen to them," his mother consoled. "You have a beautiful head. Now stop crying and go to the store for ten pounds of potatoes."

"Where's the shopping bag?"

"I haven't got one — use your hat."

大 脑 袋

"所有的孩子都拿我取乐,"小男孩哭着跟妈妈说:"他们说我长了一个大脑袋。"

"别听他们的,"他妈妈安慰说。"你的脑袋长得很漂亮。好了,别哭了,去到店里买10磅土豆来。"

"兜子在哪儿呢?"

"我没有兜子——就用你的帽子吧。"

*　　*　　*

Who Should Be Given the Present?

A father of five came home with a toy, summoned his children and asked which one of them should be given the present, "Who is the most obedient, never talks back to Mother and does everything he or she is told?" he inquired.

There was silence, and then a chorus of voices. "You play with it, Daddy!"

礼物该给谁?

一个有五个孩子的父亲带着一件玩具回到家里,把孩子们召集来问这件礼物应该给谁。"谁最听话,从不和妈妈顶嘴,让干什么就干什么?"他问道。

大家都不吭声。过了一会儿,孩子们异口同声地说:"爸爸,您玩吧。"

* * *

Two Pounds of Plums

Mother: I sent my little boy for two pounds of plums and you gave him a pound and a half.

Shopkeeper: My scales are all right, madam. Have you weighed your little boy?

两磅李子

母亲:我让小儿子来买两磅李子,可你只给了他一磅半。

店主:我们的秤准确无误,太太。您称过您的小儿子了吗?

*　　*　　*

Excited Remarks

Our son, at age five, had a fascination for motorcycles. The sight of one would always bring forth squeals of delight, accompanied by excited remarks of "Look at that! Look at that! I'm gong to have one of those someday," His dad's response always was "Not as long as I'm alive."

One day, while our son was talking to a little friend, a motorcycle passed by. He excitedly pointed it out to the boy and exclaimed, "Look at that! Look at that! I'm getting one of those as soon as my dad dies."

激动的话

我五岁的儿子对摩托车有强烈的爱好。只要看见一辆摩托车,他就会高兴得哇哇直叫,并激动地说:

"瞧这辆!瞧这辆,我总有一天也要有一辆。"他爸爸的回答老是"只要我活着,你就别想有这玩意儿。"

一天我们的儿子跟他的小朋友在说话，有一辆摩托车开了过去。他兴奋的指着摩托车叫道“瞧这辆！瞧这辆！等我爸一死我就要有这样一辆摩托车了。”

*　*　*

Visiting Patients

When my wife went in the hospital for surgery several years ago, a rule prohibited children under 12 from visiting patients. Our 11-year-old seemed to understand, but our six-year-old took the restriction very hard. We discovered why she was so unusually upset when we heard her talking to her mother on the phone for the first time. As she said good bye, she tearfully exclaimed, “I'll see you when I'm 12, Mom!”

探望病人

几年前，我妻子动手术时，医院有条规定禁止12岁以下的儿童探望病人。我们11岁的孩子似乎能理解，可6岁的女儿对此却非常伤心。等听到她头一次给她妈妈打电话，我们才明白她为何如此分外激动。在电话里，她边说再见，边哭着喊道妈妈,等我 12 岁时一定去看你!

* * *

Lucky Mother

A young mother believed that it was very wrong to waste any food when there were so many hungry people in the world. One evening, she was giving her small daughter the tea before putting her to bed. First she gave her a slice of fresh brown bread and butter, but the child said that she did not want it like that. She asked for some jam on her bread as well.

Her mother looked at her for a few seconds and then said, "When I was a small girl like you, Mary, I was always given either bread and butter, or bread and jam, but never bread with butter and jam."

Mary looked at her mother for a few moments with pity in her eyes and then said to her kindly, "Aren't you pleased that you've come to live with us now?"

幸运的母亲

一位年轻的母亲认为,世界上还有许多受饥饿的人，浪费食物真不应该。有天晚上，在安排幼小的女儿睡觉之前，她给女儿喂夜宵。她先给她一片新鲜的黑面包和黄油，但孩子说她不喜欢这样吃。她还要一些果酱涂在面包上。

母亲看了女儿几秒钟，随即说道，“玛丽，当我像你一样小的时候，总是吃面包加黄油，或者面包加果酱，从来没有面包既加黄油又加果酱。”

玛丽看了母亲一会儿，眼中露出怜悯的神情，然后她柔声说：“您现在能跟我们生活在一起难道不感到高兴吗？”

* * *

Facts of Life

I have always tried to be open and honest with my children whenever they came to me with questions, but six-year-old Peter caught me off guard one evening when he bounced in at dinner time and asked, “Mom, when you get married, does that make you pregnant?”

“No,” I answered, “Getting married is not what makes you pregnant.”

“Well,” he persisted, “how do you get pregnant then?”

Not wishing to get into such a serious

discourse just before dinner, I answered, "Peter, it's s sort of a long story."

Within an impish look on his little face, he cocked his head and replied, "You don't know, do you?"

生命知识

每当孩子们问我问题时,我总是试图坦诚相告。可是,有天晚上,我那六岁的儿子彼得把我难住了。他在晚饭时冲回家来,突然问道:"妈,结婚会使人怀孕吗?"

"不,"我说:"结婚不一定会使人怀孕。"

"那么,"他追问道:"你是怎么怀孕的?"

我不想在吃饭前讨论如此严肃的话题,于是答道:"彼得,这事儿一时半会也说不清楚。"

彼得的小脸上一副调皮模样,他歪着头说:"你也不知道,是吗?"

*　　*　　*

Personal Hero

Our granddaughter's second-grade class was asked to write about their personal heroes. Her father was flattered to find out that she had chosen him. "Why did you pick me?" he asked.

"Because I couldn't spell Arnold Schwarzenegger," she said.

心目中的英雄

我们的孙女儿读二年级,老师要求班上的同学写他们心目中的英雄。她的爸爸发现她选择了他,真是受宠若惊。"你为什么选我呢?"他问。

"因为我不会拼阿诺得·施瓦辛格(Arnold Schwarzenegger),"她说。

* * *

Synonym = Bad Language

One day a ten-year-old child asked his mother, "Mom, what is a synonym?"

"What? You even don't know what a synonym is? How foolish you are. When I describe you as foolish, I mean you're silly, stupid. Now you know what a synonym is?"

"Yes, a synonym is using bad language." The child concluded.

同义词=骂人

一天,一个十岁的孩子问母亲:"妈,什么是同义词?”

“你说什么?竟然连同义词都不懂!真是个笨蛋。我说你是个笨蛋,就是说你是个傻瓜,是个蠢货。你现在明白同义词的意思了吗?”

“明白了。同义词就是骂人。”

* * *

You Look As Your Father

Colin had just returned from college, resplendent in loudly-checked trousers, silk hosiery, a fancy waistcoat, and a necktie that spoke for itself. He entered the library, where his father was reading. The old gentleman looked up and surveyed his son. The longer he looked, the more disgusted he became.

"Son," he finally blurted out, "you look like a silly fool!"

Later the old major who lived next door came in and greeted the boy heartily.

"Colin," he said, with undisguised admiration, "you look exactly as your father did twenty-five years ago, when he came back from school."

"Yes," said Colin, with a smile. "Father

was just telling me so."

像你父亲一样

科林刚从大学回来，穿着颜色鲜艳的方格长裤、丝质袜子、精致的西服背心，以及自然分明的领带，显得容光焕发。他进入书房，他的父亲正在阅读。老绅士抬头望望他儿子，越看就越觉得厌恶。

"儿子啊，"最后他脱口而出，"你看起来像个傻子！"

后来住在隔壁的老少校进来了，热烈地跟那男孩打招呼。

"科林，"他坦然地称赞说，"你看来就像你父亲25年前从学校回来的样子。"

"是的，"科林微笑着说，"父亲刚刚还在告诉我。"

*　　*　　*

All Right

Hurrying my 11-year old daughter to school, I made a right turn at a red light when it was prohibited. "Uh-oh," I said, realizing my mistake. "I just make an illegal turn."

"I guess it's all right." my daughter replied, "The police car behind us did the same thing."

没 关 系

我赶着开车将 11 岁的女儿送到学校去，在红灯处右拐了，而那是不允许的（译注：在一些国家如英国，其交通规则是车辆左行的，与我国相反）。“啊噢，”意识到犯了错误，我说。“我刚才拐弯是违章的。”

“我想那没关系的，”女儿回答说：“我们后面的警车也同样拐了弯。”

*　　*　　*

I Didn't Notice It

Mother: I left two pieces of cake in the cupboard this morning, Jimmy, and now there is only one piece left. Can you explain that?

Jimmy: Well, I suppose it was so dark that I didn't notice the other.

我没有看到它

母亲：吉米，今天早上我在食品橱里放了两块蛋糕，现在只剩下一块了，你说是怎么回事？

吉米：哦，我想是因为里面太黑，我没有看见另一块。

*　　*　　*

Without the Money

"Sonny, did you pick up my suit from the tailor?"

"He refused to give it to me without the money, Pop."

"Didn't you tell him I thought you were too young to carry money?"

"Yeah, but he said he'll keep the shirt until I get bigger!"

没有带钱

"乖儿子,你到裁缝师那儿把我的西服拿回来没有?"

"没有钱他不肯把衣服给我,爸爸。"

"你没告诉他我认为你太小,不能带钱?"

"说了,可是他说他要保留衣服,直到我长大一点!"

* * *

What Am I Supposed to Do?

"What am I supposed to do?" a youg man looking to get married asked his friend. "Every woman I bring home to meet my parents, my mother doesn't like."

"Oh, that's easy," his pal replied. "All you have to do is find someone who's just like your mother."

"I did that already," he said, "and that one my father didn't like."

我该怎么办?

"我应该怎么办?"一位正找对象要结婚的年轻人问他的朋友,"每一个我带回去见我父母的女孩,我妈妈都不喜欢。"

"啊,这容易。"他的伙伴说,"你只要找个像你妈妈的女孩就行了。"

"我这样试过了,"他说,"可是那个我爸爸又不喜欢。"

* * *

Wow the Door Is Opened

Stepping from my kitchen into the garage, I accidentally locked myself out of the house. When I tried to persuade my 18-month-old son, Taylor, to open the door, none of my tactics worked. Finally, I walked around the house to check for an open window. To my amazement, I found the front door open and Taylor standing there with a salesman.

"I've been locked out for 20 minutes," I said. "How did you get him to open the door?"

Looking puzzled, the man replied, "I rang the door bell."

门是怎么开的

我从厨房到车库时,无意间把自己锁在了房子外。我竭力说服我 18 个月的儿子泰勒打开门,可我怎么说也没用。最后,我绕着房子转起圈,看能不能找到一扇开着的窗户,令我惊奇的是,我发现前门已经打开了,泰勒和一个推销员站在那儿。

我说:"我被锁在外面有 20 分钟了,你是怎么让他打开门的?"

推锁员一头雾水:"我是按的门铃呀。"

Ⅳ

Childishness

童　稚

The Sun and the Moon

Two boys are talking about the sun and the moon. "Which one of them is more useful?" asked one of them.

"Of course the moon is. The moon is in the sky when it's dark, but the sun is in the sky in the daytime when nobody needs it."

太阳和月亮

两个男孩在谈论太阳和月亮。“它们中哪一个更有用?”其中一个问。“当然是月亮。月亮是在天黑的时候挂在空中。可是太阳是在白天谁也不需要它的时候出现在空中。”

*　　*　　*

A Baby Sister

Nurse: Don't you like your new baby sister, Johnnie?

Johnnie: She's all right, but I wish she had been a boy. Willie Smith had got a new sister, and now he'll think I'm trying to copy him.

小　妹　妹

保育员：乔尼,你难道不喜欢你新生的小

妹妹?

乔尼:她还可以,但要是个男孩就好了。威利·史密斯先有了一个新生的小妹妹。现在他该认为我又在学他的样子了。

* * *

Whose Father Was the Stronger

Gill and Nill were quarrelling about whose father was the stronger. Gill said, "Well, you know the Pacific Ocean? My father's the one who dug the hole for it."

Nill wasn't impressed, "Well, that's nothing. You know the Dead Sea? My father's the one who killed it!"

谁的父亲更强壮

吉尔和尼尔在为谁的父亲更强壮而争吵。吉尔说:"喏,你知道太平洋吗?就是我爸爸为它挖的洞。"

尼尔不屑一顾:"噢,那没什么。你知道死海吗?那是我爸爸杀死的。"

* * *

Can His Football Come to Play?

A little boy knocked on the door of his friend's house. When his friend's mother answered, he said, "Can Dean come out to play, please?"

"No, I'm afraid not." said Dean's Mum. "It's too wet."

"Well, then," asked the lad, "Can his football come to play?"

他的足球能出来玩一会吗?

小男孩在敲他朋友家的门。他朋友的妈妈来开门了。他说:"迪安能出来玩一会儿吗?"

"不能,他恐怕不行,"迪安的妈妈说。"外面太湿了。"

"那么,"小男孩又问,"他的足球能出来玩吗?"

*　*　*

A Small Boy and a Donkey

A small boy leading a donkey passed by an Army camp. A couple of soldiers wanted to have some fun with the lad. "What are you holding onto your brother so tight for, sonny?" saked one of them.

"So he won't join the army," the youngster replied without blinking an eye.

小男孩与驴子

一个小男孩牵着头驴子穿过部队营房。两名士兵想跟小家伙开个玩笑:"小孩,你把你哥哥牵得这么紧干什么?"

"这样,他就不会去参军了。"小家伙眼都不眨地回答道。

*　　*　　*

A Girl's Wish

On the way home after watching a ballet performance, the kindergarten teacher asked her students what they thought of it. The smallest girl in the class said she wished the dancers were taller so that they wouldn't have to stand on their toes all the time.

一个小姑娘的希望

看完芭蕾舞表演,幼儿园的老师在回家的路上问她班里的孩子们感觉怎么样。班里最小的一个女孩说,她希望演员们个子再高点就好了,这样就不用老是踮着脚跳了。

*　　*　　*

That's Why

Tommy started painting when he was three years old, and when he was five, he was already very good at it. He painted many beautiful and interesting pictures, and people paid a lot of money for them. They said, "This boy's going to be famous when he's little older, and then we're going to sell these pictures for a lot more money."

Tommy's pictures were different from other people's because he never painted on all of the paper. He painted on half of it, and the other half was always empty.

"That's very clever," everyone said, "Nobody else does that!"

One day somebody bought one of Tommy's pictures and then said to him, "Please tell me this, Tommy. Why do you paint on the bottom half of your pictures, but not on the top half?"

"Because I'm small," Tommy said, "and my burshes don't reach very high."

原来如此

汤米三岁开始画画，五岁时已经画得很好了。他画了很多美丽而有趣的画，人们出高价购买。他们说，“这个孩子长大一点肯定会出名，我们可以靠这些画大赚一笔。”

汤米的画与众不同。因为他从来不在整张纸上作画。他只画一半的纸，而另一半他总空着。

“构思多么巧妙啊！”大家都说，“从来没有人这么做过。”

有一天，一个人买了汤米的画，然后问他：“请告诉我，汤米，你为什么总是在纸的下半部分画画，而不是在纸的上半部分？”

汤米说，“因为我个头小，够不着上面。”

V

Waiter and Customer

服务员与顾客

She Knew Him Now

A man called at a village post-office for a registered letter. The letter was there, but the clerk did not give it to the man. "How can I know that the letter is for you?" she said.

The man took a photograph of himself from his pocket, and said, "I think now you know who I am." The clerk looked long at the photo and then said. "Yes, that's you. Here's your letter."

她知道他是谁了

一个人来到一个村邮局取挂号信。信在那儿，但业务员不给他。"我怎么知道这封信是你的?"她说。

这个人从衣袋里掏出一张他自己的照片来说："我想你现在知道我是谁了吧。"业务员对着照片看了好一会儿说："是的，这是你本人，给你信。"

* * *

We're Both Wrong

On a flight from New York City to Geneva, Switzerland, I sat next to a passenger who spent most of the time pestering and insulting the flight attendant. Nevertheless, the latter efficiently complied with every request. Suddenly my obnoxious seatmate said, "You're the dumbest individual I've ever come across."

"And you are the most amiable I ever met," the flight attendant calmly replied. "But it is just possible that we're both wrong."

我们俩都错了

在一架从纽约飞往瑞士日内瓦的客机上，我邻座上的一位乘客对飞机上的服务员纠缠不休，并侮辱服务员。然而后者非常有效率地满足了他的每一项要求。忽然，这位可憎的邻座说："你是我遇到的最笨的人。"

"而您是我遇到的最和善的人，"服务员冷静地回答。"但是也可能是你我都错了。"

*　　*　　*

The First Flight

An old lady was making her very first flight in an airliner. She was highly nervous and insisted on speaking to the captain before take — off.

"You will bring me down safely, won't

you?" she asked anxiously.

"Don't worry, madam," said the captain cheerfully, "I've never left anyone up there yet."

第一次乘飞机

一位老太太第一次乘飞机，她的心情非常紧张，在飞机起飞前，她坚持要跟机长说句话。

“你会让我安全地下飞机的，是吧？”她担忧地问。

“别担心，夫人，”机长高高兴兴地说，“到目前为止我还没有把任何人留在上面。”

* * *

He Was Six When He Left

After waiting over three frustrating hours at the airport for the arrival of a plane that had been delayed in take-off, a man approached the boarding desk and asked for an arrival-time update. He was concerned because he was meeting his nephew and this was the boy's first flight.

"How old is the boy?" the airline representative asked solicitously.

"He was six when he left," the man replied

sharply.

他离家时六岁

因为飞机起飞延误,一个人在机场等着接人已经三个多小时了。他走近问询处打听飞机到达时间的最新消息。他非常着急,因为他是来接侄子的,而侄子是第一次乘飞机。

“男孩多大了?”航空公司的人关心地问。

“他离开家时六岁。”他不客气地回答。

* * *

One Engine Left

A 747 was halfway across the Atlantic when the captain got on the loud speaker, “Attention, passengers. We have lost one of our engines, but we can certainly reach London with the three we have left. Unfortunately, we will arrive an hour late as a result.”

Shortly thereafter, the passengers heard the captain’s voice again, “ Guess what, folks. We just lost our third engine, but please be assured we can fly with only one. We will now arrive in London three hours late.”

At this point, one passenger became furious.

"For Pete's sake," he shouted, "If we lose another engine, we'll be up here all night!"

只剩一个引擎

一架 747 客机正在跨越大西洋时,传来了机长的声音:"旅客们请注意,我们的四个引擎中有一个失效了。但剩下的三个引擎会把我们带到伦敦的,只是我们要因此晚到一小时。"过了一会儿,旅客们又听到机长的声音:"各位,你们猜怎么啦? 我们刚又失去了第三个引擎。但请你们相信好了,只有一个引擎我们也能飞,但要晚三个小时了。"正在这时,一位乘客非常气愤地说:"看在上帝的分上,如果我们再失去一个引擎,我们就要整夜呆在天上了。"

* * *

Where is the Winner?

Customer: This lobster's only got one claw.

Waiter: I guess he's been in a fight, sir.

Customer: Well, bring me the winner.

胜者在哪里?

顾客:这只龙虾只有一只爪子。

侍者:我猜应该是在打架时弄丢的,先生。

顾客：那样的话，给我那只打胜的。

*　　*　　*

The Patron and the Manager

"What's this daily charge for fruit?" the hotel patron asked the manager. "We didn't eat any."

"But the fruit was placed in your room every day. It isn't our fault you didn't take advantage of it."

"I see," said the man as he subtracted $150 from the bill.

"What are your doing?" sputtered the manager.

"I'm subtracting fifty dollars a day for your kissing my wife."

"What? I didn't kiss your wife."

"An," replied the man, "but she was there ..."

旅客和经理

"这是什么，每天都收我水果费？"旅客问经理，"我们一个也没吃。"

"可是水果每天都在您的房间，而您自己不去享受这种待遇，这就不能怪我们了。"

“我明白了。”他说着从账单里减去了 150 美元。

“你在干什么?”经理唾沫飞溅地说。

“我每天扣除五十块你吻我妻子的钱。”

“什么? 我根本就没吻过你的妻子。”

“嗯,”这人回答说,“可她也在这儿……”

* * *

The Customer Is always Right

The manager of a shop was ticking off one of his staff. “I saw you arguing with a customer,” he said crossly, “Will you please remember that in my shop the customer is always right. Do you understand?”

“Yes, sir,” said the assistant, “The customer is always right.”

“Now what were you arguing about?”

“Well, sir, he said you were an idiot.”

顾客永远正确

商店的经理正在斥责他的一个售货员。“我看见您在和一位顾客争吵,”他非常恼火地说。“你不记得了在我的店里顾客永远是正确的。你懂了吗?”

“是的，先生，”售货员说。“顾客永远是正确的。”

“你刚才为什么和他争论?”

“噢，先生，他说您是个白痴。”

* * *

The Sign Is No Need

A fishmonger was painting “Fresh Fish Sold Here Today” above his shop when a passer-by said to him, “you don’t want to put ‘Today’, do you? I mean you won’t be selling it yesterday or tomorrow, will you?”

“No, I suppose not,” said the fishmonger.

“And then you don’t want ‘Here’ either — you’re not selling it anywhere else, are you?”

“No, that’s quite right,” agreed the fishmonger.

“And then why put ‘Sold’?” continued the helpful man, “You’re not going to give it away, are you?”

“Of course I’m not,” said the fishmonger.

“And then why say ‘Fresh’ — after all, you wouldn’t sell it if it weren’t fresh, would you?”

“I certainly wouldn’t,” said the fishmonger. “I must thank you for saving me so much trouble."

"Just one final thing," said the man, "You don't need 'Fish' either — I could smell it two streets away!"

这招牌没用

一个鱼店主人正在店门上用油漆写"此处今日出售鲜鱼"的招牌。这时一个过路人对他说："你不需要写'今天'吧？我的意思是说，你不会是昨天卖或是明天卖，是不是？"

"我想不会。"鱼店主人说。

"再说，你也不需要写'此处'——你不会是在别处卖吧？"

"不会，你说得对。"鱼店主人表示同意。

"此外，为什么要写'出售'呢？"这位助人为乐的过路人又说。"你不会白白把鱼送给人吧？"

"当然不会。"鱼店主人说。

"还有，为什么写'鲜'字呢？说到底鱼不鲜你是不会卖的吧？"

"当然不会，"鱼店主人回答。"我得感谢你省了我这么些事。"

"还有最后一件事了，"那人说。"你也无需写上'鱼'字——我隔两条街就嗅到它的腥味了。"

* * *

Repair the Doorbell

Woman at door：I thought you were coming to repair the doorbell yesterday?

Repairman：I did — I rang twice but got no answer，so I went home.

修 门 铃

站在门口的主妇：我以为你是要昨天来修门铃的。

修理工：是的，我来过——我按了两次门铃，没人来开门，我就回家了。

*　　*　　*

To Save the Trouble

It was an extremely rough channel crossing from Weymouth to Jersey，and one wretched green-faced passenger was hugging the rail when a steward approached him.

"Lunch，sir?" asked the tactless steward.

"No，thanks，" groaned the passenger，"Just throw it overboard and save me the trouble ..."

省　　事

轮船横渡英吉利海峡，从韦穆特到泽西岛去，一路风浪极大。一个痛苦不堪的乘客脸色发绿，紧靠着船栏杆。这时，一个餐厅服务员走近他。

“先生，您要吃午餐吗？”不善察言观色的服务员问道。

“不吃了，谢谢你，”乘客呻吟着说，“你干脆把它倒进海里，省我一番事……”

* * *

Would that Be Satisfactory?

The salesclerk had patiently listened to the complaints of the disgruntled customer for quite some time. Finally, as she went on and on about her dissatisfaction with a purchase she had made, he politely interrupted her. “Madam, suppose we refund your money, send you another one without charge, close the store, and have the manager shot. Would that be satisfactory?”

这样满意吗？

营业员耐心地听着一位不满意的顾客发牢骚，已有好大一阵子了。最后，当她还在没完没了地说着她所购买的不满意的货品时，他有礼貌地打断了她。“夫人，假如我们退回您的货款，再白送您一件商品，商店停业，再把经理枪毙——这样您可以满意了吗?”

*　　*　　*

To Throw a Rock

While out shopping, my uncle discovered that he had forgotten his wallet and had only a few coins in his pocket. When he tried calling home, the operator asked for an additional twenty-five cents. “Twenty-five cents more!” my uncle cried. “Why, I can throw a rock from here and hit my house,” Calmly the operator replied, “In that case, sir, I suggest you tie a note to it.”

扔石头

我叔叔有一次出去买东西,发现忘了带钱包,兜儿里只有几个硬币。他想往家里打个电话,电话员要他再付25分。“再交25分?”我叔叔叫道,“我从这扔个石子儿都能打到家里。”电话员不慌不忙地说,“既然这样,先生,我建议您还是写个纸条系在石头上扔回家去。”

*　　*　　*

He's Just Been to the Zoo

When I was waiting in line at the bank, I

noticed a woman holding a small child at one of the windows. The boy was eating a roll, which he thrust at the teller. The teller smiled and shook his head.

"No, no, dear," said the boy's mother, and then, turning to the teller, "I beg your pardon, young man. Please forgive my son. He's just been to the zoo."

他刚去过动物园

当我在银行里排队时,发现一位妇女抱着一个小孩站在一个窗口。小男孩正在吃一个面包卷,并将面包卷戳向出纳员,出纳员笑着摇了摇头。

"别这样,亲爱的,"男孩的妈妈说。然后她转向出纳员说,"对不起,小伙子。请原谅我的儿子,他刚去过动物园。"

* * *

He Obeyed

The conductor wakes up a passenger, sleeping by the window.

"Your ticket, sir."

"Ticket? I have no ticket."

"No ticket? But where are you going?"

"I'm not going anywhere."

"Then why did you get on the train?"

"I was meeting a train, when you shouted: 'Please take your seats!' so loudly, that I just had to get into the carriage."

他服从了命令

列车员叫醒了睡在窗子边的旅客。

"先生,您的票?"

"票,我没票。"

"没票? 那么你去哪儿?"

"我哪儿也不去。"

"那你为什么要上车?"

"我是来接人的,当你喊:'大家都上车'时,声音那么大,吓得我不得不到车厢里来了。"

* * *

It Wasn't There This Morning

A boastful American from Texas was being shown the sights of London by a taxi-driver.

"What's that building there?" asked the Texan.

"That's the Tower of London, sir," replied the taxi-driver.

"Say, we can put up buildings like that in two weeks," drawled the Texan.

A little while later he said, "And what's that building we're passing now?"

"That's Buckingham Palace, sir, where the Queen lives."

"Is that so?" said the Texan. "Do you know back in Texas we could put up a palace like that in week."

A few minutes later they were passing Westminster Abbey. The American again asked, "Hey, cabby, what's that building over there?"

"I'm afraid I don't know, sir," replied the taxi-driver. "It wasn't there this morning!"

今天早上还没有呢！

一个从美国得克萨斯州来的爱吹牛的人乘出租车在伦敦观光。

"这是什么建筑物?"得克萨斯人问。

"先生,那是伦敦塔,"出租司机回答。

"我跟你说,在我们那儿两星期就可以建起一座这样的建筑物。"得克萨斯人拉长腔调说。

过了一会儿他又问:"我们刚才经过的是什么建筑?"

"先生,那是白金汉宫,是女王住的地方。"

“是吗?”得克萨斯人说。“你要知道在我们那儿像这样的宫殿只需一个星期就能建成。”

几分钟后他们又经过了威斯敏斯特大教堂。这位美国人又问:“嘿,司机,那边儿是什么楼?”

“先生,恐怕我也不知道,”司机说。“今儿早晨还没有呢!”

* * *

Modern Art

A very superior person was walking round an art exhibition, when he paused. “I suppose this hideous monstrosity is what they call modern art!” he told an attendant.

“No, sir,” replied the attendant, “that's what they call a mirror.”

现代艺术

一个自命不凡的人在参观一个艺术展览。他停了下来,对工作人员说:“我想这一可怕的奇形怪状的东西就是所谓的现代艺术!”

“不,先生,”工作人员回答。“这个东西就是所谓的镜子。”

* * *

He Should Be Ashamed

Said the bellhop to a noisy drinking party of collegians in a hotel bedroom: "I'v been sent to ask you to make less noise. The gentleman in the next room says he can't read."

"Tell him," was the reply of one of the revelers, "that he ought to be ashamed of himself. Why, I could read when I was five years old."

他应感到害臊

旅馆服务员对一伙在一间旅馆房间里举行晚会的大学生说:"住在隔壁房间的先生让我来告诉你们小点声,他都不能读书了。"

"告诉他,"欢饮者中的一个说,"他应该为自己感到害臊,我五岁的时候就能读书了。"

*　　*　　*

I'll See to the Rest

A guard was about to signal his train to start when he saw an attractive girl standing on the platform by an open door, talking to another pretty girl inside the carriage.

"Come on, miss!" he shouted. "Shut the door, please!"

"Oh, I just want to kiss my sister goodbye," she called back.

"You just shut that door, please," called the guard, "and I'll see to the rest."

剩下的由我来办

当一位车上的列车员刚要发出信号让火车启动时,他看见一位很漂亮的姑娘站在站台上一节打开的车厢门旁边,跟车厢里的另一位漂亮的姑娘在说话。

"快点,小姐!"他喊着。"请把车门关上!"

"噢,我还没和妹妹吻别呢,"她回答说。

"请把门关上好了,"列车员说,"剩下的事由我来办。"

*　　*　　*

You Might Be as Lucky as That Man

An insurance salesman was trying to convince a potential customer to buy insurance. "Only last week I sold a life insurance policy to a man 33 years old. The very next day he had an accident and died, and our company promptly awarded £ 100 000 to his family. Now just think — you might be as lucky as that man!"

没准你会和他一样幸运

一个保险推销员在使劲说服一位顾客去办理保险。"上个星期我给一位只有三十三岁的人办了人寿保险。第二天那人就出事故死了。我们公司立刻给他家赔偿 100 000 英镑。你想想,没准你会和他一样幸运的。"

*　　*　　*

Roses for My Wife

On the way home one night, I spotted some fresh-cut roses outside a florist's shop. After selecting a dozen and entering the shop, I was greeted by a young saleswoman.

"Are these for your wife, sir?" she asked.

"Yes," I said.

"For her birthday?" she asked.

"No," I replied.

"For your anniversary?"

"No," I said again.

As I pocketed my change and headed toward

the door, the young woman called out, "I hope she forgives you."

给妻子的玫瑰

一天晚上回家的路上,我看到一家花店外面有一些刚剪下来的玫瑰。我挑了一打,走进店里,一个年轻的女售货员跟我打了个招呼。

"先生,这些是送给你妻子的吗?"她问道。

"是的,"我说。

"她的生日?"她问。

"不是,"我回答。

"你们的结婚纪念日?"

"不是,"我又答道。

当我将找回的钱装进口袋,朝门口走去时,那年轻的女人冲我喊道:"希望她能原谅你。"

*　　*　　*

Too Polite

A woman who frequented a small antique shop rarely purchase anything, but always found fault with the merchandise and prices. The manager and her salesclerk took the woman's grumpy complaints in stride, but one day she went too far. "Why is it I never manage to get what I ask for in your shop?" demanded the woman.

A smile on her face, the clerk calmly replied, "Perhaps it's because we're too polite."

太有礼貌

一名妇女经常光顾一家小古董店，但几乎从不买什么东西，却总是对商品和价格吹毛求疵。对于那妇女的粗暴抱怨，经理和她的销售员总是应付了事，但是有一天她做得太过分了。"为什么你们店里总是不能得到我想要的东西？"那名妇女指责说。

职员脸上带着微笑，沉着地回答道："也许是因为我们太有礼貌了。"

* * *

Camera

On our way to a wedding in Vermont, my husband and I realized we had forgotten our camera. We stopped at a general store and, hoping to purchase a cheap, disposable model. Sal asked the owner, "Do you have any of those throwaway cameras?"

"Look, fella," replied the owner, "I don't care what you do with it after you buy it."

照 相 机

在前往威蒙特参加一个婚礼的路上，我和丈夫意识到我们忘了带照相机。我们在一家百货商店前门停了下来，希望能够买到一种便宜的，一次性照相机。萨尔问店主："你们有那种用了就扔的照相机吗？"

"我说，小伙子，"店主回答说，"我可不管你买了之后怎么处理它。"

Ⅵ

Employer and Employee

老板和雇员

A Clever Answer

At a job interview, my husband was asked if he would mind working under the direct supervision of a woman. "I am British," he replied, "We have a queen in the throne, we have a female prime minister and I have been married for more than 30 years. I know how to take orders from a woman."

He got the job.

聪明的回答

在一次寻求工作的面试中,人家问我的丈夫是否愿意在一位女领导的手下干事。他回答:"我是英国人,我们的国家有女王,首相也是女首相,何况我结婚已三十多年了,我知道怎么去执行女士们的命令。"

他得到了工作。

*　　*　　*

Mixed up

"Are you still working in that florist's?"

"No, I got the sack."

"Why?"

"I had to put the cards into the floral tributes and I got two of them mixed up. The flowers going to a wedding I thought were going to a funeral, so I put in a card which read 'With Deepest Sympathy...' and the flowers going to the funeral had a wedding card in them."

"What did it say?"

"Hope You'll Be Happy in Your New Home!"

搞 混 了

"你还在那家花店里工作吗?"

"不,我被解雇了。"

"为什么?"

"我得在每束花里放一张卡片,结果我把两张卡片搞混了。我把那束送人婚礼的花错以为是送人葬礼的花,所以我放进了一张卡片,上面写着'致以深深的吊唁……'而那束送人葬礼的花里放了一张新婚贺卡。"

"上面写的是什么?"

"愿你在新的家庭里幸福美满!"

* * *

Midway Tactics

Three competing store owners rented

adjoining shops in a mall. Observers waited for mayhem to ensue.

The retailer on the right put up huge signs saying, "Gigantic Sale!" and "Super Bargains!"

The store on the left raised bigger signs proclaiming, "Prices Slashed!" and "Fantastic Discounts!"

The owner in the middle then prepared a large sign that simply stated, "ENTRANCE".

中间战术

三个互相争生意的商店老板在一条商业街上租用了毗邻的店铺。旁观者等着瞧好戏。

右边的零售商挂起了巨大的招牌，上书："大减价！""特便宜！"

左边的商店挂出了更大的招牌，声称："大砍价！""大折扣！"

中间的商人随后准备了一个大招牌，上面只简单地写着："入口处"。

* * *

Two Tunnels

When the British government let out bids for the digging of a tunnel under the English

Channel, estimates ran in the millions of pounds. One firm asked only 10, 000 pounds however.

"Considering equipment and labor costs," the construction chairman asked the low bidder, "how do you propose to do the job for such a pittance?"

"It's simple," the contractor replied "My partner grabs a shovel, goes to France and starts digging. I take another shovel and start digging from England. We dig until we meet — and you've got a tunnel!"

"But what if you never meet!"

"Then you've got two tunnels."

两条隧道

英国政府招标要在英吉利海峡底下挖一条隧道，估计需耗资几百万英镑。然而，一个公司仅投标10 000英镑。

工程主席问这位低价投标人："考虑一下设备和人力，用这么少的资金你打算怎么挖这条隧道？"

"这很简单，"承包人回答。"我的搭档抓起一把铁锹，到法国去挖，我也抓起一把铁锹从英国开始挖。等我们俩会合了，你们的隧道就成功了！"

"如果你们碰不到怎么办?"

"那你们就有了两条隧道。"

* * *

It's Not an Accident

A country lad was being interviewed for a farm labourer's job.

"You must be fit," said the farmer. "Have you had any illnesses?"

"No, sir," said the lad.

"Any accidents?"

"No, sir."

"But you walked in here on crutches," said the farmer. "Surely you must have had an accident?"

"Oh, that!" replied the lad, "I were tossed by a bull — but it wasn't an accident, sir. He did it on purpose!"

不是意外事故

一位乡下小伙子想到一个农场去干体力活,正在接受面试。

"你的身体一定健康吧,"农场主说,"你有什么病没有?"

“没有，先生，”小伙子回答。

“发生过意外事故吗？”

“没有，先生。”

“可你是拄着拐杖来的，”农场主说，“肯定是遇到过意外事故。”

“啊，是这样！”小伙子回答，“我被一头公牛撞了一下，可这不是什么意外事故，先生，它是故意这样做的！”

* * *

Call Again

“What job are you doing now?”

“I’m a debt-collector.”

“That’s not a very pleasant job, is it?”

“Oh, I don’t know. People are always asking me to call again.”

下次再来

“你现在做什么工作呢？”

“我现在是个催债员。”

“这工作可不怎么样，是吧？”

“嗯，不见得吧。人家总是跟我说下次再来。”

* * *

The Clerk Grows a Beard

"Sir," said the manager to a clerk, "you must go to the barber and get a shave."

"But , sir," protested the clerk, "I am growing a beard."

"Do what you like at home," said the manager, "but you mustn't grow a beard during office hours."

职员留胡子

"先生,你得到理发店去修修面。"经理对一个职员说。

"但是,先生,我正在留胡子。"那个职员争辩说。

"你在家里爱干什么就干什么,"经理说,"但你不能在上班时间留胡子。"

*　*　*

A New Employee

Several weeks after a young man had been hired, he was called into the personnel director's office.

"What is the meaning of this?" the director

asked. "When you applied for the job, you told us you had five years' experience. Now we discover this is the first job you ever held."

"Well," the young man said, "in your advertisement you said you wanted somebody with imagination."

一位新雇员

一位被雇用了几个星期的年轻男士被叫到人事处处长的办公室。

处长问:"这是什么意思? 你申请工作时对我们说你已经有五年的工作经验,现在我们发现这是你的头一份工作。"

"哦,"那位年轻男士答道:"你们的招聘广告上说你们需要有想象力的人才呀。"

Ⅶ

Doctor and Patient

医生和病人

I Can Do Nothing

One's wife could not read the thermometer, but she took her husband's temperature with it and gave a call to the doctor. "Dear Doctor, please come at once. My husband's temperature is 63."

The doctor replied, "Dear Madam, I can do nothing. Send for the fire brigade."

我无能为力

一位妻子不会看体温表。她量了丈夫的体温后给医生打电话说:"亲爱的医生,请快来吧。我丈夫的体温是 63 度。"医生回答说:"亲爱的太太,我无能为力了,您叫消防队吧。"

* * *

Get the Cat out First

"Doctor, doctor!" said the panic-stricken woman, "my husband was asleep with his mouth open, and he's swallowed a mouse! What shall I do?"

"Quite simple," said the doctor calmly. "You just tie a lump of cheese to a piece of string and lower it into your husband's mouth. As soon as the mouse takes a bite — haul it out."

"Oh, I see. Thank you, doctor. I'll go round to the fishmonger straight away and get a cod's head."

"What do you want a cod's head for?"

"Oh — I forgot to tell you, I've got to get the cat out first!"

先把猫引出来

"医生,医生!"一位惊慌的妇女叫喊着,"我的丈夫张着嘴睡觉时,吞进了一只耗子!我该怎么办呢?"

"这容易,"医生平静地回答。"你把一小块干酪用线绳系上吊到你丈夫的嘴里,当耗子咬上一口时你一拉线绳就出来了。"

"噢,我明白了。谢谢您,医生,我马上去鱼商那里弄个鱼头来。"

"你弄个鱼头有什么用?"

"噢——我忘了告诉您,我得先把猫引出来!"

*　　*　　*

Rabies

Doctor: I'm sorry to tell you, but you have

rabies.

Patient: Quick, give me a pencil and paper.

Doctor: Do you want to write your will?

Patient: No — I want to make a list of all the people I intend to bite.

狂 犬 病

医生：我很遗憾地告诉你，你得的是狂犬病。

患者：请快给我一支铅笔和一张纸。

医生：你要写遗嘱吗？

患者：不——我要把我存心要咬的人列个名单。

* * *

Don't Do Anything Rash

Patient: I've decided to commit suicide.

Psychiatrist: Don't do anything rash until you've paid my bill!

不要鲁莽从事

患者：我决定要自杀。

精神病医生：在没有付清我的治疗费之前，不要鲁莽从事。

* * *

To Pay In Advance

"I'm always forgetting things," the distraught man grumbled to the psychiatrist. "What should I do?" "The first thing to do," the doctor prescribed, "is pay me in advance."

先 付 钱

"我老是忘掉事情，"心烦意乱的人对精神病医生抱怨说，"我该怎么办？""第一件要做的事，"医生指示说，"就是先付钱。"

* * *

Lost Memory

Patient: I've lost my memory.

Doctor: When did this happen?

Patient: When did what happen?

失去记忆力

患者：我失去记忆力了。

医生：这事是什么时候发生的？

患者：什么事是什么时候发生的？

* * *

The First Operation

Patient: I'm so frightened — this is my first operation.

Surgeon: I know just how you feel — this is my first operation, too.

第一次手术

患者：我太害怕了——因为这是我第一次动手术。

外科医生：我理解你——这也是我头一次动手术。

*　*　*

The Vision Had Not Yet Healed

An old woman was suffering from an eye disease and she sent for the doctor. He promised her that he would not charge anything for the medicine needed for her eyes if they did not recover, but if they were cured, she would have to pay the sum that he requested. The doctor went to her house every day and treated her eyes medically. He was such a mean man that every time he went to her house, he would take home something that belonged to her without her knowledge. In a month her eyes were completely cured, so the doctor asked her to cover the cost of the medicine. But the demand was refused, for she said her vision had not yet healed as she could not yet see all her furniture.

视力未恢复

有个老太太罹患眼疾，请了个医生来。医生对她承诺，如果万一她的眼睛没复原的话，就不收取任何医药费，可是如果医好了，她就是付他要求的所有费用。医生每天到她家里，去为她的眼睛做药物治疗。他是个很卑鄙的家伙，每次到她家，都未经许可拿走属于她的东西。一个月后，她的眼睛完全治好了，因此医生便要求她付医药费。但是这项要求被拒绝了，因为老太太说，她看不到她所有的家具，这证明她的视力仍然没有恢复。

* * *

Delusion

Psychiatrist: Congratulations, Mr. Jones. You're finally cured of your delusion. But why are you so sad?

Patient: Wouldn't you be sad if yesterday

you were President of the United States and the next day you were nobody?

幻 想 症

精神病医生：恭喜你，琼斯先生。你终于治好了你的幻想症。但是你为什么如此悲伤?

病人：如果你昨天是美国总统，第二天变成了无名小卒，你不会难过吗?

* * *

The Fat Man

A doctor advised a very fat man to take up golf for exercises. "That's no good to me," said the patient, "I've tried it before. If I put the ball where I can hit it I can't see it, and if I put where I can see it I can't hit it!"

胖 子

大夫劝告一位很胖的人把打高尔夫球作为减肥运动。"那对我不合适，"患者说。"我从前试过。如果我把球放在我能打着的地方，我就看不见球。反过来，我要把球放在能看见的地方，我又打不着了!"

* * *

To Give up Smoking

"I went to my doctor to see if he could help me to give up smoking."

"What did he say?"

"He suggested that every time I felt like a smoke I should reach for a bar of chocolate."

"Did that do any good?"

"No — I can't get the chocolate to light."

戒 烟

"我去看了医生,想让他帮我戒烟。"

"医生怎么说?"

"他建议每当我想抽烟时就伸手拿一块巧克力。"

"这个办法怎么样?"

"不行——巧克力点不着。"

* * *

Get Me a Video

A man unable to stop himself stealing asked the doctor for help and advice.

"Try these pills," said the doctor. "They should help."

"But what if they don't?" asked the wretched patient.

"Then see if you can get me a video, will you?"

给我弄一台录像机

有一个人没办法控制自己偷东西的毛病，就去求医生帮助。

"先吃这些药片试试，"医生说。"应该会见效的。"

"如果不见效怎么办？"可怜的病人问。

"那就给我弄一台录像机，好吗？"

* * *

Send the Bill to My Father

Doctor: "I can do nothing for your complaint. It is hereditary."

Patient: "Then send the bill to my father, please."

把账单给我父亲

医生："对你的抱怨我无能为力。那是遗传病。"

病人："那请你把账单给我父亲吧。"

* * *

Good News and Bad News

An artist asked the gallery owner if anyone had shown interest in his paintings. "I've got good news and bad news," she said. "The good news is that some guy inquired about your work and wondered if it would appreciate in value after you died. When I told him it would, he bought all 15 of your paintings."

"And the bad news?"

"The guy was your doctor."

好消息和坏消息

一位艺术家问美术馆馆长是否有人对他的画感兴趣。"有好消息也有坏消息,"她说。"好消息是有一个人询问你的作品并想知道你死后这些作品能否增值。当我告诉他可以增值,他便将你15幅画全部买下了。"

"那么坏消息呢?"

"那个人就是你的医生。"

Ⅷ

viii

Police

警　察

I'm Not Daft

A policeman was escorting a prisoner to gaol when his hat blew off. "Shall I run and get it for you?" asked the prisoner obligingly.

"You mustn't think I'm daft," said the constable. "You stand here and I'll get it."

我 不 傻

一个警察押送一个犯人去监狱。忽然他的帽子被风吹掉了。"我跑去替您捡帽子,行吧?"犯人讨好地问。

"你以为我那么愚蠢吗?"警官说,"你站在这儿我去捡。"

* * *

To Get Home before an Accident

"Why were you speeding, madam?" asked the traffic cop.

"Well, officer," came the reply, "my brakes are bad and I wanted to get home before I had an accident."

在出事前赶回家

"夫人,你为什么要超速行驶?"交通警察问。

“噢,警官,”那位妇女回答说,“我的刹车坏了,我想在出事前赶到家。”

*　　*　　*

Police Hospitality

I was surprised to learn that my 72-year-old mother dared to drive 900 miles in a 12-year-old car to visit me. When asked how she made out, she told me just fine — until her second night. She had filled the gas tank and didn't have the money for a motel room.

“What did you do!” I asked.

“Well,” she began, “I was driving through this small town and feeling very sleepy. A policeman pulled me over and asked if I had been drinking. When I told him no, he wanted to know why I was weaving all over the road. I explained my situation. ‘Follow me,’ he ordered. We then drove to a motel where the nice officer paid for the night's lodging.”

“As he was leaving,” Mother continued, “he turned to me and said, ‘Ma'am, the next time you have to visit your daughter, please take another route.’”

警察的款待

我非常惊奇地得知我七十二岁的老母竟然开着一辆已用了十二年的旧车，行驶九百多英里来看我。当我问她一路上是否平安无事，她告诉我起初很好，一直到第二天晚上，她在加油站装满了油箱后，没钱住旅馆了。

“您怎么办的呢?”我问道。

“嗯，”她说，“我驾车在这个小城镇里穿过去，感到很困。一位警察把我叫到马路边停下，问我是否喝醉了。当我告诉他没有时，他问我为什么在马路上左拐右转地开车。我给他讲了我的情况，他说：‘跟我来。’然后我们来到了汽车旅馆，这位善良的警官为我付了一夜的住宿费。”

“当他离开时，”妈妈继续说：“他转过身对我说，‘夫人下次再去看女儿时，请走另一条路线。’”

* * *

Reached Shore Fast

A guy I know was towing his boat home from a fishing trip to Lake Huron when his car broke down. He didn't have his cell phone with him, but he thought maybe he might be able to raise someone on his marine radio to call for roadside assistance. He climbed into his boat, clicked on the radio and said, "Mayday, mayday." A Coast Guard officer came on and said, "State your location." "I-75, two miles south of Standish." After a very long pause, the officer asked, "How fast were you going when you reached shore?"

快速靠岸

在休伦湖钓完鱼后，我的一个朋友开车拖着他的船回家。路上车坏了。他没带手机，不过，他想，也许他可以通过海事无线广播来请求公路援助。于是，他爬到他的船里面，启动了无线装置，喊道，"求救，求救"。一名海岸护卫队警官作出了回应，"报告你的位置。""I-75 号公路，Standish 的南面两英里"。沉默了好一会之后，警官问我的朋友，"你的船靠岸时开得有多快？"

* * *

A Smuggler

The suspicious-looking man drove up to the border, where he was greeted by a sentry. When the guard looked in the trunk, he was surprised to find six sacks bulging at the seams.

"What's in here?"he asked.

"Dirt," the driver replied.

"Take them out," the guard instructed. "I want to check them."

Obliging, the man removed the bags, and sure enough, each one of them contained nothing but dirt. Reluctantly, the guard let him go.

A week later the man came back, and once again, the sentry looked in the truck.

"What's in the bags this time?" he asked.

"Dirt, more dirt." said the man.

Not believing him, the guard checked the sacks and, once again, he found nothing but soil.

The same thing happened every week for six months, and it finally became so frustrating to the guard that he quit and became a bartender. Then one night, the suspicious-looking fellow happened to stop by for a drink. Hurrying over to him, the former guard said, "Listen, pal, drinks are on the house tonight if you'll do me a favor: Just tell me what the hell you were smuggling all that time."

Grinning broadly, the man leaned close to the bartender's ear and whispered, "Cars."

走 私 犯

一个形迹可疑的人开车来到边境，哨兵迎了上去。哨兵在检查汽车行李箱时，惊奇地发现了六个缝得紧绷绷的大口袋。

“里面装的是什么？”他问道。

“土。”司机回答。

“把袋子拿出来”，哨兵命令道：“我要检查。”

那人老老实实地把口袋搬了出来。一点不假，口袋里除了土什么也没有。哨兵很不情愿地让他通过了。

一周后，那人又来了，哨兵再次检查汽车上的行李箱。

“这次袋子里装的是什么？”他问道。

“土，又运了一些土。”那人回答。

哨兵不相信，对那些袋子又进行了检查，除了土仍旧一无所获。

同样的事情每周重演一次，一共持续了六个月。最后，哨兵被弄得灰心丧气，干脆辞职去当了酒吧侍者。有天晚上，那个形迹可疑的人碰巧到那里喝酒。那位前哨兵急忙迎上前去对他说，“我说，老兄，你要是能帮我一个忙，今晚的酒就归我请客。你能不能告诉我，那段时间你到底在走私什么东西？”

那人俯身过来，凑近侍者的耳朵，咧开嘴笑嘻嘻地说：“汽车。”

IX

Soldier

军　人

What's your name?

A very strict officer was talking to some new soldiers whom he had to train. He had never seen them before, so he began: "My name is Stone, and I'm even harder than stone, so do what I tell you or there'll be trouble. Don't try any tricks with me, and then we'll get on well together."

Then he went to each soldier one after another and asked him his name. "Speak loudly so that everyone can hear you clearly," he said, "and don't forget to call me 'sir'".

Each soldier told him his name, until he came to the last one. This man remained silent, and so Captain Stone shouted at him, "When I ask you a question, answer it! I'll ask you again: What's your name, soldier?"

The soldier was very unhappy, but at last he replied. "My name is Stonebreaker, sir." he said nervously.

你叫什么名字?

有一位很严厉的军官在对一群交由他训练的新兵训话。他以前从没见过这群新兵,于是他开始自我介绍："我的名字叫 Stone（石头），事实上，我甚至比石头更强硬。这就是我为什么要告诉你们我名字的原因。不要试图对我玩什么花招，这样我们就能很好相处了。"

接着他开始走到每个士兵前面问他们的名字。"说大声点，让每个人都能听清楚。另外，不要忘记称呼我为长官。"他说。

每个士兵都对他说了自己的名字。他走到最后一位士兵面前时，这个士兵保持着沉默。于是 Stone 队长对他喊叫，"当我问你问题的时候，要回答！我再问一遍，你的名字，士兵？"

那个新兵很不高兴，但最后他回答了。"我的名字是 Stonebreaker（碎石机），长官。"他紧张地说。

*　　*　　*

Visual Training

The squad were having "visual training". One smart recruit was asked by the officer to count how many men composed a digging party in a distant field. The party was so far away that the men appeared as mere dots, but unhesitatingly the recruit replied:

"Sixteen men and a sergeant, sir."

"Right; but how do you know there's a

sergeant there?"

"He's not doing any digging, sir."

视力训练

班里正在进行"视力训练"。一个聪明伶俐的新兵被班长叫出来数远处旷野上采掘队的人数。采掘队在很远的地方,那些人看起来只是一些小点儿。但是这个新兵毫不犹豫的回答:

"十六个士兵和一个中士,长官。"

"正确。可你如何知道那儿有一个中士?"

"他不干活,长官。"

* * *

Five Months Older

The Second World War had begun, and James wanted to join the army, but he was only 16 years old, and boys were allowed to join only if they were over 18. So when the army doctor examed him, he said that he was 18.

But James' brother had joined the army a few days before, and the same doctor had examed him too. This doctor remembered the older boy's family name, so when he saw James' papers, he was surprised.

"How old are you?" he asked.

"Eighteen, sir," said James.

"But your brother was eighteen, too." said the doctor, "Are you twins?"

"Oh, no sir," said James, and his face went red. "My brother is five months older than I am."

大 五 个 月

第二次世界大战开始了,詹姆斯想去当兵。可他只有十六岁,当时规定男孩到十八岁才能入伍。当军医给他进行体检时,他说他已经十八岁了。

可詹姆斯的哥哥刚入伍没几天,而且也是这个医生给他做的检查。这位军医还记得他哥哥的姓。所以当他看到詹姆斯的表格时,感到非常惊奇。

"你多大了?"军医问。

"我十八了。"詹姆斯说。

"可是你哥哥也刚十八岁,你们是双胞胎吗?"

詹姆斯脸红了,说:"不是,先生,我哥哥比我大五个月。"

* * *

I Didn't Know That I Was So Far Back Already!

A big battle was going on during the First

World War. Guns were firing, and shells and bullets were flying about everywhere. After an hour of this, one of the soldier decided that the fighting was getting too dangerous for him, so he left the front line and began to go away from the battle. After he had walked for an hour, he saw an officer coming towards him. The officer stopped him and said, "Where are you going?"

"I'm trying to get as far away as possible from the battle that's going on behind us, sir." the soldier answered.

"Do you know who I am?" the officer said to him angerly. "I'm your commanding officer."

The soldier was very surprised when he heard this and said, "My God, I didn't know that I was so far back already!"

真没想到我已经往回跑了这么远!

第一次世界大战期间,一场大战役正在进行。枪炮轰鸣,子弹横飞。这样持续了一小时后,有个士兵认为战斗太危险了,所以他离开前线,开始逃离战场。走了一个小时后,他看见一个军官朝他走过来。军官拦住他,问道:"你到哪儿去?"

"长官,我正尽力躲开身后正在进行的战斗。"

士兵回答说。

"你知道我是谁吗?"军官生气地说:"我是你们的指挥官。"

士兵听了十分惊讶地说:"天哪,真没想到我已经往回跑了这么远!"

* * *

The Same Duties

A retired four-star general ran into his former orderly, also retired, in a Manhattan bar and spent the rest of the evening persuading him to come work for him as his valet. "Your duties will be exactly the same as they were in the army," the general said. "Nothing to it, you'll catch on again fast."

Next morning promptly at eight o'clock, the ex-orderly entered the ex-general's bedroom, pulled open the drapes, gave the general a gentle shake, strode around the other side of the bed, spanked his employer's wife on her bottom and said, "OK, sweetheart, it's back to the village for you."

相同的职责

一个退休的四星级将军在曼哈顿的一个酒吧

偶然地遇到了他以前的勤务兵，勤务兵也退休在家。这位将军花了一整个晚上的时间来说服他回来做他的贴身随从。"你的职责与在军队时完全一样，"将军说，"这没什么，你很快就会再次理解它的。"

第二天早晨八点钟时，前勤务兵迅速地进到前将军的卧室，拉开窗帘，轻轻地摇了摇将军，然后大步走到床的另一侧，在他雇主的妻子屁股上拍了一下，说道："好了，甜心，你该回到村庄去了。"

* * *

Nobody Listens

General John Galvin, Supreme Allied Commander in Europe and Commander-in-Chief of U. S. European Command, was asked what was it like to be in charge of so many and various forces.

His reply, "I often feel like the director of a cemetery. I have a lot of people under me, but nobody listens."

谁也不听我的

约翰·加尔文将军曾任欧洲盟军最高统帅和美国驻欧军队总指挥，有人问他，指挥这么多不同国家的部队是什么滋味。

他回答说:“我常觉得像是公墓的管理员。底下的人很多,可是谁也不听我的。”

* * *

Very Pleased to Meet You

During World War Ⅱ, a lot of young women in Britain were in the army. Joan Phillips was one of them. She worked in a big camp, and of course met a lot of men, officers and soldiers.

One evening she met Captain Humphreys at a dance. He said to her, "I'm going abroad tomorrow, but I'd be very happy if we could write to each other." Joan agreed, and they wrote for several months.

Then his letters stopped, but she received one from another officer, telling her that he had been wounded and was in a certain army hospital in England.

Joan went there and said to the matron, "I've come to visit Captain Humphreys."

"Only relatives are allowed to visit patients here," the matron said.

"Oh, that's all right," answered Joan. "I'm

his sister."

"I'm very pleased to meet you," the matron said, "I'm his mother!"

很高兴认识你

在第二次世界大战中，有许多年轻的妇女在军营中服役。琼·菲利浦斯是其中之一。她在一个大军营中工作，当然遇到了许多男士，包括军官和士兵。

一天晚上她在舞会上遇到了军官汉弗雷斯。他对她说，"我明天就要出国，但如果我们能够相互写信，我会很高兴。"琼同意了，于是他们几个月里一直通着信。

后来，他再没有来信。她收到了另一个军官的信，告诉她，他受伤了，住在英格兰的某个部队医院里。

琼到了医院，她对护士长说，"我来看望军官汉弗雷斯。"

"这里只有亲属可以探望病人。"护士长说。

"噢，是的，"琼说，"我是他的妹妹。"

"很高兴认识你，"护士长说，"我是他的母亲。"

* * *

None Other Than a Soldier

As a newly commissinaed infantry lieutenant,

I was eager to set an example for my platoon by cleaning my own M－16 rifle. While we were working on the weapons, one soldier complained about the unusual notched shape of the M－16's bolt and chamber, which makes it difficult to clean.

"Lieutenant, they need to make something to clean this with," the soldier said.

"They do," piped up a sergeant.

"Really," I said with surprise, wondering why we had not ordered such a tool.

"Yes, sir," replied the sergeant. "It's called a soldier."

正是士兵

作为一名新上任的步兵中尉，我通过擦拭自己的 M－16 式自动步枪给全排作个榜样。我们一块擦枪，一名战士抱怨由于 M－16 的枪栓枪膛的特别凹形结构，擦起来十分困难。

"中尉，应该制造一种擦这枪的工具。"士兵说。

"已经制造出来了。"一军士尖叫。

"真的?"我十分诧异，纳闷为什么我们没有订购这种工具。

"真的，长官，"军士答道，"它就是士兵。"

X

Celebrity

名　　人

Albert Einstein's Overcoat

One day the famous scientist Albert Einstein came across an old friend of his in a street in New York.

"Mr. Einstein," said the friend, "it seems that you need to have a new overcoat. Look, how worn out it is."

"It doesn't matter," answered Albert Einstein. "No one knows me here in New York."

Several years later, they met in New York again. Einstein had become a world-famous physicist by then, but he still wore the same old overcoat. Once more his friend tried to persuade him to buy a new one.

"There's no need now," said Einstein. "Every body here knows me."

阿尔伯特·爱因斯坦的大衣

一天,著名的科学家爱因斯坦在纽约的大街上碰到了他的一位老朋友。

"爱因斯坦先生,"朋友说,"看来你需要换一件新大衣了。瞧,这件已经穿坏了。"

"没关系,"阿尔伯特·爱因斯坦回答。"在纽约没人认识我。"几年过去之后,他们又在纽约相遇。这时爱因斯坦已是世界闻名的物理学家了。但他仍穿着那件旧大衣。他的朋友又一次试图劝他换件新的。

“现在没有必要了,”爱因斯坦说。“这儿的每一个人都认识我了。”

* * *

Einstein and Charlie Chaplin

Einstein was a great admirer of Charlie Chaplin's films. Once, in a letter to Chaplin he said:“I admire you very much. The ‘Modern Times’ everybody in the world can understand. You will certainly become a great man. Einstein.”

In his answer to this letter Charlie Chaplin wrote:“I admire you even more. Your Theory of Relativity nobody in the world understands, but you have already become a great man. Chaplin.”

爱因斯坦和查理·卓别林

爱因斯坦非常喜欢查理·卓别林的电影。他在一封给卓别林的信中写道:“我很敬佩您。全世界的人都看得懂您的电影‘摩登时代’。您必将成为一位伟人。爱因斯坦。”

卓别林在给爱因斯坦的回信中写道:“我更敬

佩您。全世界没有一个人懂得您的相对论,但您已经成为伟人了。卓别林。”

* * *

Bootblack

A foreign diplomat, according to Lincoln folklore, came upon Lincoln while he was polishing his shoes. “What, Mr. President,” he cried, “you black your own boots?” “Yes,” said Lincoln. “Whose do you black?”

擦皮鞋的人

根据民间关于林肯的传说,有一位外国外交官偶然见到林肯正在擦皮鞋。他叫道:“噢,总统先生,你自己擦皮鞋?”“是的,”林肯说,“那么你给谁擦皮鞋呢?”

* * *

Done Enough

A woman imperiously demanded a colonel's commission for her son. “Sir,” she told Lincoln, “My grandfather fought at Lexington, my father fought at New Orleans, and my husband was killed at Monterey." "I guess, madam," said Lincoln, "your family has done enough for the country. It's time to give somebody else a chance."

贡献够大了

一位妇女蛮不讲理地要求任命她的儿子为陆军上校。她对林肯说:"先生,我祖父在列克星敦打过仗,我父亲在新奥尔良战斗过,我丈夫战死在蒙特雷。""我认为,太太,"林肯说,"你们家对国家的贡献够大了,该给别人一个机会了。"

* * *

Jack London and the Editor

Jack London was late in delivering a story which he promised a New York magazine.

The editor, after repeated efforts to get the story, at last called at London's hotel and sent up the following note:

"Dear Jack London: If I don't receive the story within twenty-four hours, I'll come up to your room and kick you downstairs, and I always keep my promises."

London replied: "Dear Dick, If I did all my work with my feet, I'd keep my promises, too."

杰克·伦敦与编辑

杰克·伦敦答应为纽约的一家杂志社送去一篇小说稿,但过期未交。编辑经过了多次努力想得到小说稿。最后他去伦敦住的旅馆拜访他,在条子上写下了这样一句话,叫人送上楼去:“如果我在二十四小时内还拿不到小说稿,我会到你的房间把你从楼上踢下楼去,我总是说话算数的。”

伦敦写条子回答说:“亲爱的迪克,如果我是用我的双脚工作的话,我也是说话算数的。”

*　　*　　*

A Bad Work of Nature

When Whistler had finished a portrait of a well-known celebrity, he asked him whether he liked it.

“No, I can’t say I do, Mr. Whistler, and you must really admit it’s a bad work of art.”

“Yes,” replied the artist, looking at his sitter through his monocle, “but then you must admit that you are a bad work of nature.”

大自然的一件糟糕的作品

惠斯勒为一位知名人士画完肖像后,他问那个人是否喜欢这幅肖像。

“不,我无法说我喜欢它,惠斯勒先生。你不能不承认这是一件糟糕的艺术作品。”

“对,”惠斯勒一面透过单片眼镜看着被他画像的人,一面答道“可是您也得承认,您自己是大自然的一件糟糕的作品。”

*　　*　　*

Something for Everybody

One day Lincoln was ill and not inclined to listen to people nagging him for jobs. Just as one of these pests had seated himself for a long interview, the President's physician happened to enter the room. Lincoln, holding out his hands, asked him, “Doctor, what are those blotches?” “That's varioloid, or mild small-pox,” said the doctor. “They're all over me,” said Lincoln. “It is contagious, I believe?”

“Very contagious, indeed,” aid the doctor Lincoln's visitor got up at this point and exclaimed, “Well, I can't stop now, Mr. Lincoln. I just called to see how you were.” “Oh! don't be in a hurry,” Lincoln said. “sir”, said the visitor hastily, “I'll call again.” And he headed for the door. “There is one good thing about this,” remarked Lincoln as the man left, “I now have something I can give everybody.”

可以给任何人的东西

一天，林肯生病了，他不想听那些人跟他唠叨求职的事。这时正有一个这样讨厌的人刚刚坐下了，准备进行长时间的面谈。总统的医生碰巧进了房间。林肯伸出手问：“医生，这是什么疙瘩？”医生说：“这是微痘症，是一种假型天花。”林肯说：“我浑身都是，我想，这会传染的吧？”医生说：“传染得非常厉害。”在这个节骨眼上，林肯的客人站了起来，大声说：“噢，我不能再待下去了，林肯先生。我只是来看看你怎么样了。”“哎，别着急，”林肯说。这位客人慌慌忙忙地说：“先生，我还会来看你的。”他向门口走去。这人走后，林肯说：“这病有一个好处，我现在有一样东西了，谁要我都可以给。”

*　　*　　*

My Father Isn't as Rich as His

This is a story about the well-known millionaire, John D. Rockefeller, and was told by a friend of his. This friend said that though Rockefeller gave away millions, he was very mean about small sums of money. One day he went to stay at a hotel in New York and asked for the cheapest room they had. Rockefeller said, "What is the price of the room?" The manager told him.

"Is that the lowest priced room you have? I am staying here by myself and only need a small room."

The manager said, "that room is the smallest and cheapest we have," and added, "But why do you choose a poor room like that? When your son stays here he always has our most expensive room; yours is our cheapest." "Yes," said Rockefeller, "but his father is a wealthy man; mine isn't."

我爸爸不如他爸爸富有

这是著名百万富翁约翰·D·洛克菲勒的一个朋友讲的关于他的事。他的这位朋友说虽然洛克菲勒把上百万元的钱捐赠出去,但他对一笔笔小钱却是非常吝啬的。一天他来到纽约的一家旅馆,要住最便宜的房间。洛克菲勒问道:"你们最便宜的房间一晚多少钱?"经理告诉了他。

"这是你们最便宜的房间吗?我是一个人住,只需要一间很小的房间。"

经理说:"这就是我们最小最便宜的房间。"他又说:"您为什么要住这样简陋的房间?您儿子在我们这里住时，从来都是住最贵的房间。您却要住最便宜的房间。”“是的，”洛克菲勒说，“他爸爸是个富翁，但我爸爸不是。”

* * *

Alfred Smith's Speech

Soon after Alfred Smith was elected governor of New York for the first time he went to Sing Sing to visit the state prison. After being shown the buildings by the warden, the governor was asked to speak to the inmates. He was embarrassed, having never spoken to the inmates of a prison before, and did not quite know how to begin. Finally he said, "My fellow citizens," Then he remembered that when one goes to the state prison he is no longer a citizen. So the governor was even more embarrassed, and said: "My fellow convicts!" That did not sound just right, so Alfred said, "Well, anyhow, I'm glad to see so many of you here."

阿尔弗雷德·史密斯的讲话

阿尔弗雷德·史密斯被选为纽约州州长后不久第一次去参观设在星星的州立监狱。看守人员向他介绍了监狱的建筑物之后，要求他给犯人讲几句话。因为他从没给犯人讲过话，有点窘迫，不知道该怎么开始。后来，他说道："公民同胞们，"这时他忽然想起来，进了州立监狱的人已不再是公民了。这时，这位州长就显得更加的难堪了。他又说道："囚犯同胞们！"这句话听起来也不是很恰当，于是阿尔弗雷德说："噢，无论怎样，我很高兴能在这里见到你们这么多人。"

* * *

Goethe's Tolerance

Goethe was once strolling on a narrow path in a park in Weimar. As luck would have it, he met with a critic who was hostile to him. Both of them stopped, staring at each other. Then the critic said, "I'll never make way for a fool." "But I will," with that Goethe retreated aside.

歌德的容忍

一次，歌德正在魏玛一个公园的一条狭窄小道上散步。碰巧他遇见一个对他怀有敌意的评论家。两人都停了下来，彼此相互对视。接着评论家说道："我从来不给傻瓜让路。""可我让。"说完，歌德退到了一边。

Ⅺ

Others

其 他

PET
SHOP

A Bad Impression

Six people were travelling in a compartment on a train. Five of them were quiet and well behaved, but the sixth was a rude young man who was causing a lot of trouble to the other passengers.

At last this young man got out at a station with his two heavy bags. None of the other passengers helped him, but one of them waited until the rude young man was very far away and then opened the window and shouted to him, "You left something behind in the compartment!" Then he closed the window again.

The young man turned around and hurried back with his two bags. He was very tired when he arrived, but he shouted through the window, "What did I leave behind?"

As the train began to move again, the passenger who had called him back opened the window and said, "A very bad impression!"

一个坏印象

有六个人搭乘火车旅行,坐在同一车厢内。其中五个很安静,也很规矩。但第六个是个粗鲁的年轻人,给其他乘客招惹了许多麻烦。

最后，这位年轻人在一个车站带着两个沉重的皮箱下了车。没有一个旅客帮他的忙。有个人一直等到这位粗鲁的年轻人走得很远了，才打开窗户，对着他大声喊："你把东西留在车厢里了!"然后，又把窗户关了起来。

年轻人转过身子，拎着两个沉甸甸的皮箱，匆匆赶了回来。他转回来时，显得非常疲倦，对着窗户大声喊："我把什么东西留在车上了?"

当火车再次启动时，叫他回来的旅客打开窗户说："一个极坏的印象!"

* * *

A Good Lesson

It was Sunday. The train was crowded. A gentleman was walking along the platform looking for a place. In one of the cars he saw a vacant seat. But a small suit-case was lying on it and a young man was sitting next to it.

"Is this seat vacant?" asked the gentleman.

"No, it is my friend's," answered the young man. "He is just coming, this is his suit-case."

"Well," said the gentleman, "I'll sit here till he comes". Five minutes later the train started, but nobody came. "Your friend is late," said the gentleman. "He had missed his train, but he need not lose his suit-case." And with these words he took the suit-case and threw it out of the window. The young man got up and tried to catch the suit-case, but it was too late. It was his suit-case and he had taken a second seat for his own comfort.

一次深刻的教训

星期天,火车上非常拥挤。一位先生沿着站台走并向车里看,想找一个座位。在一节车厢里他看到一个空座位。可是有一只小提箱放在上面。一位年轻人坐在旁边。

"这是个空座位吧?"这位先生问道。

"不,是我朋友的,"年轻人回答,"他马上就来,这是他的提箱。"

"好吧,"这位先生说,"我先坐在这儿,等他来了我就走。"五分钟过去了,火车启动了,还没有人来。"你的朋友晚了。"这位先生说,"他赶不上车了,但他没有必要也丢了手提箱。"说着他拿起箱子扔出了窗外。这位年轻人站了起来企图抓住箱子,可是已经晚了。箱子就是他的。他用箱子占了个座位,本想使自己更舒服点。

*　　*　　*

Queue-Jump

My aunt is never happy when she has to wait in line, and people who try to squeeze in front are a special sore point with her.

One day a young man at the supermarket stepped up to her just as she reached the checkout counter. "Mind if I go ahead?" he asked. "I just have this one can of dog food."

"Goodness, no," she roared. "If you're that hungry, go right ahead!"

加塞儿

我的婶婶最不情愿排队等着买东西，那些设法加塞儿的人对她来说就更可气了。

一天我婶婶在超级市场里买东西，她刚排到收款台前时，一个年轻人走上来说："我在您的前面您介意吗?"他说，"我只买了这一罐狗食罐头。"

"天啊，我不介意，"她喊叫着。"你如果真饿成那样，就先买吧!"

* * *

Jerome Makes a Complete Apology

One evening a young man at Oxford who

was known to be something of a poet read one of his poems to a small group of friends in his room. The poem was greatly admired, but as they came away one of the friends, Jerome, said, "I was very much interested in Alfred's poems but it was stolen from a book."

This remark was repeated to Alfred, who was very annoyed and demanded an apology.

"Well," said Jerome, "I don't often take back what I have said, but on this occasion I admit I was mistaken. When I got to my room I looked in the book from which I thought the poem was stolen — and I found it was still there."

杰罗姆的道歉

在牛津大学，一天晚上，一位被认为多少是个诗人的年轻人在他的房间里给他的几位朋友读他的一首诗。他的诗得到了很高的赞美。他们告辞后，一位名叫杰罗姆的朋友说："我对阿尔弗雷德的诗很感兴趣。可他这是从一本书上偷来的。"

这话传到了阿尔弗雷德耳朵里。他很气恼，并要求查尔斯道歉。

杰罗姆说："嗯，一般说，我说出去的话不再收回。但这次我承认，是我搞错了。我本认为他从那本书里偷走了这首诗，但当我回到房间里找出那本书时，发现那首诗还在里面。”

* * *

I'm Not Swimming

A naughty lad was swimming in a private part of the river when the owner spotted him.

"Hey!" he bawled, "You can't swim here!"

"I'm not swimming," the lad shouted back, "I'm stopping myself sinking!"

我不是游泳

一个顽皮的小伙子在一条河的私人区里游泳时被主人发现了。

“嘿!”他喊道，“别在这儿游泳!”

“我不是在游泳，”小伙子喊道，“我是在使自己别沉下去。”

* * *

Keep It Secret

Carl and Henry met in the street one day.

"I want to ask you for a favour, but can you

keep it secret for me?" said Carl.

"Certainly I can," answered Henry.

"I'm short of money these days. Will you please lend me some?"

"Oh, don't worry," Henry said. "I'll take it as if I did not hear you."

保　密

有一天，卡尔和亨利在大街上相遇。卡尔说："我想请你帮我个忙，但你能替我保密吗？"

"当然能，"亨利回答。

"这些日子我缺钱，请你借我一些好吗？"

"噢，别担心，"亨利说，"我就只当什么也没听见一样。"

*　*　*

A Check for Fifteen Dollars

Three men, Mr. A, Mr. B and Mr. C, each owed five dollars to a certain man. When the man died, the three decided to pay their debt at once. Mr. A put a $5 bill into the coffin, Mr. B did likewise. Mr. C put into the coffin a check for fifteen dollars and took the ten dollars in change.

一张十五美元的支票

有三个人,某甲,某乙和某丙。每人都欠同一个人五美元。那个人死后,这三个人决定立刻还债。甲往棺材里放了五美元的纸币,乙也放了五美元。丙往棺材里放了一张十五美元的支票,拿回了那十美元现钞。

*　　*　　*

The Soprano and the Contralto

Soprano: Did you notice how my voice filled the hall last night?

Contralto: Yes, dear; in fact, I noticed several people leaving to make room for it.

女高音歌手和女低音歌手

女高音歌手:你注意到昨天晚上我的嗓音是如何充满了大厅的吗?

女低音歌手:是的,亲爱的。实际上我看到几个人离开大厅是为了给你的声音让出地方。

*　　*　　*

Cat and Mice

Mrs. Watson went to visit one of her friend

and carried a small box with holes punched in the top.

"What's in your box?" asked the friend.

"A cat," answered Mrs. Watson. "You see I've been dreaming about mice at night and I'm so scared! This cat is to catch them."

"But the mice are only imaginary," said the friend.

"So is the cat," whispered Mrs. Watson.

猫和老鼠

沃森夫人去拜访一位朋友,她拿着一个顶部扎满了小眼儿的盒子。

"盒子里装的是什么?"朋友问道。

"一只小猫,"沃森夫人回答说,"你知道我晚上睡觉总梦见老鼠,我非常害怕。这只猫可以抓住那些老鼠。"

"可老鼠都是假想的呀。"朋友说。

"小猫也是假想的。"沃森夫人小声说道。

* * *

Nothing to Nothing

He and she came to the stadium when the second half had already begun.

He：What's the score?

A Man：Nothing to nothing.

She：Wonderful，we haven't missed anything!

零 比 零

当她和他来到体育场时，下半场比赛已经开始了。

他问：现在的比分是多少？

另一观众说：零比零。

她说：太棒了，我们什么也没漏掉看！

* * *

New Discovery

A hillbilly was visiting the big city for the first time. Entering an office building，he saw a pudgy older woman step into a small room. The doors closed，lights flashed，and after a while the door slid open and a beautiful young model stepped off the elevator.

Blinking in amazement，the hillbilly drawled，"I should have brought my wife!"

新 发 现

一个乡下人第一次到大城市游逛。他走进一

座大楼,看见一个岁数很大的矮胖女人迈进一个小房间。房间的门随后关上,有几个灯在闪亮。一会儿,门开了,电梯里走出一位年轻漂亮的女模特。

乡下人惊奇地眨着眼睛,慢吞吞地说:“我应该把我的老婆带来!”

*　　*　　*

What is time to a pig?

One day a visitor from the city came to a small rural area to drive around the country roads, see how the farms looked, and perhaps to see how farmers earned their living. The city man saw a farmer in his yard, holding a pig up in his hands, and lifting it so that the pig could eat apples from an apple tree. The city man said to the farmer, “I see that your pig likes apples, but isn't that quite a waste of time?” The farmer replied, “What is time to a pig?”

时间对猪有什么意义?

一天,有一个城市里的游客来到一个小乡村,在乡间路上开着车,想看看农庄是什么样子,也想看看农夫怎样种田过日子。这位城里人看见一位农夫在宅后的草地上，手中抱着一头猪，并把它举得高高的，好让它能够吃到树上的苹果。城里人对农夫说，“我看你的猪挺喜欢吃苹果的，但是，这不是很浪费时间吗？”那位农夫回答说，“时间对猪有什么意义？”

*　　*　　*

Patience

Angler: You've been watching me for three hours now. Why don't you try yourself?

Onlooker: I haven't got the patience.

耐　心

钓鱼者：你看我钓鱼看了三个小时了。你为什么不自己试一试？

旁观者：我没有那种耐心。

*　　*　　*

The Clever Parrot

A poor man had a parrot whose name was Poll. The parrot could say the words: "There is no doubt about it." He knew these words very well and called them out the whole day, "There is no doubt about it."

To every question Poll gave the same answer.

One day his master went to the market. He wanted to sell the parrot, "Who will buy my parrot?" he cried. "Twenty pounds for a clever parrot!"

The price was very high, and a man who wanted to buy him said, "Poll, are you worth twenty pounds?"

"There is no doubt about it!" was Poll's answer, so the man bought the bird, and carried him home.

Some time later he felt sorry for his money. Once he came up to the cage of the parrot, and said, "What a fool I was to throw so much money away!"

"There is no doubt about it!" cried the bird. And this time the parrot was right.

聪明的鹦鹉

一个穷人有一只名叫波尔的鹦鹉。这只鹦鹉会说:"毫无疑问。"这句话它记得很清楚,而且每天从早到晚不停地叫,"毫无疑问。"

对无论什么问题,波尔都这么回答。

一天,主人把它带到集市上去卖,"谁买我的鹦鹉?”他叫道,“二十英镑能买一只聪明的鹦鹉!”

价钱太贵了,一个买主想买,他说:“波尔,你值二十英镑吗?”

波尔回答:“毫无疑问。”买主买下了它,带回家里。

过了一段时间,这位买主觉得钱花得有点亏,他来到鹦鹉的笼子前说:“我白扔了那么多钱,真是个傻瓜!”

鹦鹉叫道:“毫无疑问!”这次它算是说对了。

* * *

The Rich and the Learned

A rich man, it is said, once asked a learned man why was it that men of science were so often to be seen at the doors of the rich, though rich men were very rarely seen at the doors of the learned.

"It is ," replied the scholar, "because the man of science knows the value of riches, and the rich man does not always know the value of science."

富人和学者

据说有一次,一个富人问一个学者,为什么人们常常在富人门口看到有学问的人，而很少在有学问的人门口看到富人。

学者回答说："这是因为学者知道财富的价值，而富人却很少知道学问的价值。"

* * *

A Compassionate Heart

A poor man once came to a millionaire and started telling him his troubles. He described his poverty so vividly that the millionaire was affected as never before. With tears in his eyes he called his servant and said to him:

"Harry, put this fellow out, he is breaking my heart."

同情的心

一个穷人来看一个百万富翁，开始向他述说他的困境。穷人生动地讲述了自己贫困潦倒的处境，竟使这位百万富翁生平第一次深受感动。他眼里含着泪水叫来仆人，吩咐他说：

"哈瑞，把这家伙给我赶出去，他使我的心都碎了。"

* * *

Early Shopper

It was Christmas and the judge was in a benevolent mood as he questioned the prisoner. "What are you charged with?" he asked.

"Doing my christmas shopping early," replied the defendant.

"That's no offense," replied the judge, "How early were you doing this shopping?"

"Before the store opened," countered the prisoner.

采购过早

那天是圣诞节,法官在审讯犯人时也有点恻隐之心。"你为什么而被起诉?"他问。

"采购圣诞节物品过早。"被告答。

"这不算犯法,"法官回答,"你购物多早?"

"在商店开门之前,"犯人应道。

* * *

A Better Offer

A commercial flight was experiencing considerable turbulence. One first-time traveler began praying. "Lord," he said, "I'm a rich man. If you just let this plane land safely, I'll give you half of everything I own."

The plane landed, and this gentleman was the first one off. In the terminal, a preacher tapped him on the shoulder. "Sir," he said, "I was on that plane with you, and I heard your prayer. Well, I'm a man of the cloth and I'm here to collect."

"I made the Lord a better offer," the rich man said. "I told him if he ever catches me on a plane again, he can have it all!"

许了更好的愿

一架民用飞机遇到了很大的湍流，有一个第一次坐飞机的旅客开始祈祷。"上帝，"他说，"我是一个富翁。如果您能使这架飞机安全降落，我将把我的财产给您一半。"

飞机降落了。这个绅士第一个走下飞机。在候机楼里，一个传教士在这人的肩上拍了一下。"先生，"他说，"我刚才和你同在那架飞机上，我听到了你的祈祷。我是传教士，现在要请你兑现诺言了。"

"我另给上帝许了个更好的愿，"这富翁说。"我告诉他如果下次能再在飞机上看到我，我的全部财产都给他。"

* * *

Play Outside

Did you hear about the young boy who was making a nuisance of himself playing in the aisle of an airplane? One of the passengers was so annoyed she finally told the boy, "Listen — why don't you go and play outside?"

到外边去玩

你听过这个故事吗？一个小男孩在飞机的走道里玩，使人讨厌，一位乘客烦得无法忍耐了。她跟小男孩说："听着——你为什么不去外面玩一会儿？"

* * *

The Damn Doors

In a parking lot, I was surprised to see a woman trying to open the door of my car. As I approached, she went to the other side, put her key in that lock and looked bewildered. "Excuse me," I said, "but that's my car." She looked around questioningly, and then spied her vehicle a short distance away. "I'm glad this one isn't mine," she replied. "I can't get the damn doors open!"

该死的车门

在停车处，我吃惊地看到一个妇女正在设法开我的车门。当我向她走近时，她走到了车的另一边，把钥匙伸进另一边的锁里，样子非常迷惑不解。“对不起，”我说，“这是我的车。”她诧异地看了看周围，发现她自己的车在不远的地方。“我很高兴这不是我的车，”她说，“这该死的车门锁坏了。”

* * *

Socks

With three men in the family, keeping socks separate is a problem. I solved the difficulty by sewing the owner's initial in bright thread on each toe.

At the gym one day, my husband was dressing when another exerciser glanced over at his feet. An "L" for Lawrence was stitched on one sock and an "R" for Robert on the other. With an amused look, the man commented, "I always thought socks were ambidextrous."

袜　子

家里有三个男人，要使袜子不搞乱很成问题。

我在每双袜子的脚趾部分用色彩鲜明的线绣上袜子主人名字的第一个字母。这样便解决了这一难题。

有一天在体育馆里，我丈夫正在穿衣服，另一个锻炼的人瞥见了他的脚。一只袜子上绣着“L”，指劳伦斯。另一只袜子上绣着“R”，指罗伯特。那个人感到很有趣，他告诉我丈夫说：“我过去还以为袜子是不分左右脚的呢。”

［注］平常一对东西注上 L 和 R 时，L 指“左(left)”，R 指“右(right)”。

* * *

Twins

“My girlfriend's one of twins.”

“How can you tell them apart?”

“Her brother's got a beard.”

双 胞 胎

“我的女朋友是一对双胞胎中的一个。”

“那你怎么辨认出哪个是她呢？”

“她哥哥长着胡子。”

* * *

Habit

Waiting in the elevator's corner, I watched with fascination as a woman got on, pushed "2" and then "4". The elevator ascended, stopping at both floors but she didn't get off.

"You missed your floor," I commented.

"I'm going to the twenty-fourth floor."

"But you pushed 'two' and 'four'."

"Oh, no," she wailed. "I've been on the computer too long!"

习　惯

我在电梯的一角里站着迷惑地看着一位夫人上了电梯,按下了"2",又按下了"4"。电梯上升了,在两层都停下了。可是她不下去。

"您错过您的楼层了,"我说。

"我要去 24 层。"

"可是你按下了'2'和'4'。"

"噢,错了",她叫道,"我搞计算机时间太久了。"

*　*　*

Mrs. P's Bathtub

Mrs. P, a refined woman in our town, was

selling some furnishings at a community auction. She pointed out the good features of each piece to the auctioneer before the sale, dwelling particularly on a shiny porcelain bathtub. "As you can see, there are no stains or scratches," she told him. "Point that out to the buyers!"

The auctioneer took her words to heart, for when the tub came up for sale he announced: "Next item is Mrs. P's bathtub — hardly been used at all."

P夫人的浴缸

P夫人是我们镇子上一位高雅的女人。她在社区拍卖一些家具。她把家具的优点在拍卖前一件件地说给拍卖商听，她特别强调了一件光亮的瓷制浴缸，"你可以看到，上面没有污点或刮痕，"她告诉他。"把这些告诉买主！"

拍卖商把她的话记在心里了，当轮到卖这只浴缸时他宣布："下一件是P夫人的浴缸，几乎没有使用过。"

*　　*　　*

You Look Perfectly Fit to Me

The distinguished old man was being

interviewed by a journalist. “I understand, sir,” said the journalist, “that you have just celebrated your ninetieth birthday?”

“That is correct — ninety years of age and I haven’t an enemy in the world.”

“That’s wonderful, sir.”

“Not an enemy in the world. They’re all dead!”

“Well, sir, I hope to have the privilege of interviewing you on your one hundredth birthday.”

“I don’t see why not, young man,” said the eminent personage, “You look perfectly fit to me!”

我看你还很健壮嘛!

记者在采访一位尊贵的老者。记者说:“先生,我知道您刚刚过了九十大寿。”

“是的,——九十岁了,我在这个世界上没有一个仇人。”

“那真太棒了,先生。”

“没有一个仇人还活在世上,他们都死了!”

“先生,我希望我能荣幸地在您一百岁大寿时再来采访您。”

“年轻人,我看没什么不行的,”这位著名人士说,“我看你还很健壮嘛!”

* * *

Why Do I Live?

Ned, a young poet, sent some verses entitled "Why Do I Live?" to the editor of a magazine. It is reported the editor replied, "You live just because you happened to send your poem by mail instead of bringing it in person."

我为什么活着?

一位叫内德的青年诗人将几首题为“我为什么活着?”的小诗寄给一家杂志出版社的编辑去发表。据说编辑回信说:“你活着是因为碰巧稿子是通过邮局寄来的,而不是你亲自送来的。”

* * *

A Heavy Sleeper

The preacher was vexed because a certain member of his congregation always fell asleep during the sermon.

As the man was snoring in the front row one Sunday, the preacher determined he would teach him not to sleep during the sermon. So, in a whisper, he asked the congregation. "All who want to go to heaven, please rise."Everyone got up except the snorer. After whispering "Be seated", the minister shouted at the top of his voiced, "All those who want to be with the devil, please rise."

Awaking with a start, the sleepy-head jumped to his feet and saw the preacher standing tall and angry in the pulpit, "Well, sir," he said, "I don't know what we're voting on, but it looks like you and me are the only ones for it."

瞌睡者

牧师非常生气,因为总有一个人在他说教时打瞌睡。一个星期天,正当坐在前排的那个人又在瞌睡时,牧师决定要好好教育他一下,让他不要再在布道时睡觉。于是他低声对信徒们说:"想去天堂的人,都请站起来吧。"所有的人都站了起来——当然,除了那个打瞌睡的人。在低声说过请坐后,牧师高声喊道:"想去下地狱的人请站起来!"打瞌睡的人被这突然的喊叫声惊醒了,他站了起来,看到牧师高站在教坛上,正生气的看着他。这个人说道:"噢,先生,我不知道我们在选什么,但看上去只有你和我是候选人。”

*　　*　　*

A Miracle

An old woman at the customs was asked if she had anything to declare.

“No, nothing at all.”

“But, what is in the bottle?”

“Oh, only holy water, holy water from the Vatican.”

The customs officer pulled the cork. “It's whiskey,” he said.

“Glory be to God!” cried the offender. “A miracle!”

奇　迹

有个老太太在海关被问到是否有东西要申报。

“没有，什么都没有。”

“但是这瓶子里装的是什么？”

“哦，只是些圣水，从梵蒂冈拿回来的圣水。”

海关人员拔开软木瓶塞，“这是威士忌，”他说。

“天啊！”违规者大叫，“真是奇迹！”

*　　*　　*

Wearing the Wrong Boots

A man went out with the wrong boots, one with a thick sole and the other with a thin one. As he began to walk, he felt uncomfortable, for one foot was higher than the other. He felt this strange and said, "Is there something wrong with my legs today? Why is one of my legs long, and the other short?"

A passerby told him that he was wearing the wrong boots. He looked down and found that it was really so. He hastily asked his servant to go back home and get another pair.

In a little while the servant ran back empty-handed. "There's no need to change them," he said. "The pair at home is the same, one with a thick sole and the other with a thin one."

穿错了鞋

一个人出门穿错了鞋子,一只鞋子底厚,一只鞋子底薄,走起路来一脚高一脚低,很不舒服。他感到很奇怪,说:"莫非今天我的腿出毛病了?为什么一条腿长一条腿短?"

一个过路的人告诉他是鞋子穿错了。他低头看了看,发现果然如此,忙让仆人回家去取另一双鞋子。

一会儿仆人空着手跑回来说:“不用换了,家里的两只也是一只底厚一只底薄。”

*　　*　　*

Why Not Build the City in the Country?

A town-dweller was visiting the country and was praising the cleanliness of the air.

“So healthy to breathe!” he exclaimed. “No pollution like the city.”

“Ar,” replied a local, “I can't understand why they don't build the city in the country!”

我为什么不把城市建在乡村?

一个城里的居民到乡下去游玩。他特别赞赏那里洁净的空气。“呼吸这样的空气对身体有好处,”他说,“不像城里空气有污染。”

“啊,”一个当地人说,“我不明白为什么不把城市建在乡村里!”

*　　*　　*

The Creative Imagination of Painters

A well-known Royal Academician who noticed

a drawing of a fish by a pavement-artist asked the man what sort of fish it was supposed to be.

"A shark, sir!"

"But you've never seen a shark," said the R. A.

"That's true, sir," the man agreed, "but then don't some of those Academy chaps paint angels?"

画家的创造性想象力

有位著名的皇家艺术院院士注意到一位马路画家画的一幅关于鱼的画，就问他，他画的可能是哪一种鱼。

"鲨鱼，先生！"

"但是您从来没有见过鲨鱼呀！"院士说。

"是的，先生，"马路画家赞同地说，"但是，一些皇家艺术院的家伙不是在画天使吗？"

* * *

Age

A guy walked into a bar and ordered a glass of 5-year-old brandy. The bartender promptly gave him his drink. After taking a sip, the man told the bartender that he had given him 1-year-old brandy. The bartender apologized and poured him another drink. The man took a sip and complained to the bartender that he had given him 3-year-old brandy. The bartender apologized and poured him another drink. The man took a sip and replied to the bartender that this was 5-year-old brandy.

Having overheard the conversation, an elderly man replied, "You sure do know your brandy." The man proudly said, "I like to think so." The old man asked if he would taste his drink and tell him the age.

"Sure," he replied and began to take a sip.

Quickly, the man spit out the drink and yelled, "This is not brandy! It's pee!"

"Yep," replied the elder, "now tell me how old I am."

年　龄

一个小伙子走进酒吧，要了一杯五年酿的白兰地，侍者很快上了他要的酒，他呷了一口，然后告诉侍者：这酒是一年酿的。侍者致歉后又上了一种。小伙子呷了一口，抱怨说侍者上的是三年酿的。侍者致歉后又换了一种。呷了一口，他告诉侍者说这才是五年酿的。

一个老头不经意间听到他们的对话，于是便说："你果真知道你这酒是哪年酿的？"

这个人骄傲地说："我想是这样。"

老头问他能否品尝一下他的饮料并说出年限。

"当然可以，"他答道并饮了一口。

很快地他又吐出来大声说道："这不是白兰地！这是尿！"

"是的，"老头答道，"现在告诉我，我今年多大岁数了？"

* * *

Drunk

Six men who were feeling no pain were staggering down the street about one in the morning. Laughing and singing loudly, they walked up to a two-story home. One of them managed to make it to the door and pounded on the doorbell insistently. A light came on in an upstairs window.

The spokesman for the group yelled up, "Is this where Mr. Brown lives?"

"Yes, it is. What do you want?"

"Are you Mrs. Brown?"

"I am Mrs. Brown. What do you want?"

"Could you come down here and pick out Mr. Brown so the rest of us can go home?"

喝 醉 了

大约凌晨一点钟,6 个已毫无知觉的人在大街上踉踉跄跄地走着。他们笑着、唱着,来到一座两层楼房前。其中一个人吃力地来到门跟前连续地按门铃。楼上窗户的灯亮了。

这个人作为他们的代表大声说:"这是布朗先生家吗?"

"是的,你想要干什么?"

"你是布朗太太吗?"

"是的。你想要干什么?"

"你能下来将你丈夫挑出来吗,我们好回家?"

* * *

A Million Dollars

A: I had a lovely dream last night; I dreamt I had a million dollars.

B: What did you do with it?

A: I put it in the bank before I woke up.

一百万美元

A:昨晚我做了个甜美的梦;我梦到我有 100

万美元。

B：你把那钱怎么办啦？

A：在我醒来之前，我把它放进银行里了。

* * *

The Light Is a Lot Better Here

One night, a man on his way home happened upon a drunk, down on his hands and knees searching for something under a street light. The man asked the drunk what he was looking for so diligently and the drunk said he had tripped and his Radar wrist watch had broken loose from his wrist. The man, being a kind-hearted soul, got down on his hands and knees and began assisting the drunk looking for his watch. After about ten minutes without any success, the man asked the drunk exactly where he tripped.

"About half a block up the street," the drunk said.

"Why, pray tell me," the man asked the drunk, "are you looking for your watch here if you lost it half a block up the street?"

The drunk replied, "The light is a lot better

here."

这儿光线好

一天晚上，一个人在回家的路上遇见一个醉汉，此人双膝跪地，正借着路灯在寻找东西。这个人问他在费力地找什么。醉汉答道，他被绊倒了。他的雷达表的表链磕松了，表从腕上掉了下来。这个人是个好心肠，也跪下来帮他找。大约十分钟过去了，还没找到。这个人问醉汉他在哪儿摔倒的。

"离这条街大约半个街区远的地方。"醉汉说。

"那么请问，你在半个街区远的地方丢的表，为什么在这儿找呢？"

醉汉答道："这儿光线好。"

《情感过山车》［英］克劳迪娅·哈蒙德著　刘文荣等译
定价：18 元

本书从科学的角度对人类的九种基本情感——喜悦、悲伤、厌恶、愤怒、恐惧、妒忌、爱情、愧疚、希望——逐一进行了考察和研究，旨在解读这些基本情感的起因。本书同时探讨了大脑和身体是如何协调一致产生各种情感的，以及我们究竟怎样才能驾驭自己的情感。作者还对人类情感中所包含的生理、心理、社会和历史等多种因素作了分析。

《世界经典故事 99》
王意如著　定价：19 元

人这种动物出现在地球上已经有五六十万年了，每天所发生的事情如恒河沙数，可为什么大部分的事情过去就过去了，有些事情却留存了下来，而且可能是永远？

上帝之手究竟拨动了人类哪一根隐秘的心弦，使这些故事具有如些神奇的力量，不管是时代的变迁还是地域的遥远，都无法抹掉它那熠熠动人的光彩？

这里的故事和写在这些故事之后的评点，或许能让你明白，什么是真正的经典故事。